FOR EDUCATION

FOR EDUCATION
TOWARDS CRITICAL
EDUCATIONAL
INQUIRY

Wilfred Carr

Open University Press
Buckingham · Philadelphia

Open University Press
Celtic Court
22 Ballmoor
Buckingham
MK18 1XW

email: enquiries@openup.co.uk
world wide web: http://www.openup.co.uk

and

325 Chestnut Street
Philadelphia, PA 19106, USA

First Published 1995
Reprinted 1998

A catalogue record of this book is available from the British Library

ISBN 0 335 19186 X (pbk)   0 335 19187 8 (hbk)

Library of Congress Cataloging-in-Publication Data

Carr, Wilfred.
    For education: towards critical educational inquiry/Wilfred
Carr.
        p. cm.
    Papers previously published in various journals between 1980 and
1989.
    Includes bibliographical references (p.) and index.
    ISBN 0–335–19187–8 ISBN 0–335–19186–X (pbk.)
    1. Education–Research.   2. Education—Philosophy.   3. Critical
theory.   4. Critical pedagogy.   5. Action research in education.
I. Title.
LB1028.C288 1995
370´.78—dc20   94–22209
                                                    CIP

Typeset by Dorwyn Ltd, Rowlands Castle, Hants
Printed in Great Britain by Biddles Ltd, Guildford and King's Lynn

For Marisse, Esther,
Sophie and Esyllt

CONTENTS

PREFACE

Books consisting of papers written by a single author are often viewed with a cynical eye. It would appear that the authors of such books are guilty of the academic sins of vanity and pride: implying that independently written papers have a collective significance that transcends their individual merits and warrants giving them a second life. In my own case, evidence of guilt abounds. The papers included in this book were written at different times and for different audiences; they are unequal in their philosophical rigour and depth; and most of them have already been published. All I can do by way of a defence is to show what brings these papers together and why it is that the book is more than the mere sum of its individual parts.

The book is intended to be a contribution to the ongoing debate about the aims and character of educational inquiry. It seeks to add a distinctively philosophical voice to this debate by concerning itself with the presuppositions of educational inquiry rather than with its methods or techniques, to lay bare and assess the theoretical grounds on which contemporary approaches to educational theorizing and research have been erected and to examine whether the study of education should be regarded as a 'science'.

The chapters of the book are divided into two parts. Those in Part I focus on a range of philosophical issues concerning the nature of educational theory, the nature of educational practice and the relationship between the two. In general terms, they reveal a dissatisfaction with the conventional way of drawing the theory–practice distinction and argue the case for treating educational theory and educational practice as mutually constitutive and dialectically related domains. The chapters in Part II offer a detailed philosophical critique of the epistemological and ideological foundations of orthodox educational research and show how developments in the philosophy of science and the philosophy of the social sciences provide new answers to old questions about the limits and possibilities of a genuinely *educational* science. In particular, they develop a detailed philosophical justification for reconstructing educational theory and research as a critical educational science: a form of educational inquiry designed to empower teachers to reconstruct their practice as an *educational* practice through a process of reflective understanding and rigorous critique.

In pursuing these ambitious aims I have tried to articulate my ideas in a clear and explicit way. But underlying and informing all my ideas is an allegiance to a particular vision of education that is not so easy to articulate: not a 'philosophy' or a 'theory' of education but a view of education as standing in a particular relationship to philosophy and theory. This understanding of education permeates every page of this book and provides the main justification for its publication. It will, therefore, be appropriate for me to speak of it here.

'Philosophy' always stands in a paradoxical relationship to 'education': it is at once its critique and one of its possibilities. To be able to undertake a philosophical critique of education is already to have acquired that level of intellectual independence and critical consciousness that education has itself made possible. To think reflectively and critically – and hence 'philosophically' – *about* education is thus always to presuppose an allegiance *to* education. It is for this reason that Plato's *Republic* can be read as a treatise both on the educational purpose of philosophy and on the philosophical purpose of education. For what Plato so clearly saw was that education in the true sense of the term is the process through which people acquire that kind of philosophical enlightenment that will emancipate them from the dictates of ignorance, dogma and superstition. As portrayed in the *Republic*, philosophy is the ultimate end of education as well as the means to its critical understanding and transformation.

If the relationship between philosophy and education is always paradoxical, the relationship between theory and education is always exasperating. To begin with, there are at least two quite different approaches to the meaning of 'theory' in the history of Western thought. As Stephen Kemmis makes clear in the Prologue to this book, one of these can be traced back at least as far as Sir Isaac Newton and receives its clearest articulation and justification in twentieth-century positivism. Within this tradition, a theory is a generalization, a set of principles, a coherent body of explanatory knowledge that can be used to predict, control and dominate the world. The value and validity of such theory is determined by its performance: by what it does, what it produces and how it can be applied. On this view, the acid test for any *educational* theory is always the practical use to which it can be put and it is judged weak or strong according to its capacity to control and guide educational practice.

The other way of understanding 'theory' has a much longer and larger historical pedigree. Like our understanding of 'philosophy' it can be traced back to Plato and, in more modern times, to ideas, values and assumptions deriving from that complex eighteenth-century configuration known as the Enlightenment. Fundamental to this view is the realization that the aim of theory is understanding and that theorizing is the distinctively human and humanizing social process through which we understand ourselves and the social world in which we live. 'Theorizing' is thus an integral part of the dialectical process of self-transformation and social change: the process through which individuals can simultaneously remake themselves and their social life. So understood, the task of theory is not to transform the world but to transform the theorist: to illuminate the basic concepts and presuppositions on which our common sense understanding of everyday life has been erected. *Educational* theory, on this view, entails grasping the values, concepts and presuppositions that structure everyday educational practice. To the extent that it involves that kind of reflexive thinking which is prepared to turn back upon itself, it has an unavoidable philosophical orientation. And to the extent that it is concerned to change education by making the educator a better 'theorist', it is itself an educative process, transforming educational practice by educating the educational practitioner. It is, then, an educational theory not because it produces 'objective' theoretical knowledge about education but because it produces precisely the kind of reflectively acquired self-knowledge that educators, *qua* educators, aspire to develop and promote in others. So understood, an educational theory is not a theory '*about* education' but a theory '*for* education', incorporating a commitment to the aims of enlightenment and empowerment that a reflexive understanding of education unavoidably entails.

That all the chapters in this book are, in some sense or other, concerned to defend forms of educational theory and research that are 'for education' rather than 'about education' largely explains its title. But it has to be admitted that the title is also a deliberate allusion to Alvin Gouldner's seminal text *For Sociology*, which was itself a response to Louis Althusser's *For Marx*. Gouldner began his book with the following quotation:

> Just as the sharpest critics of Marxism have usually been Marxists, the keenest critics of sociology have usually been sociologists and students of sociology. Often enough the men whose rejection of such criticism is most vehement are those who live *off* sociology, while the most vehement critics are those who live *for* it. Often, but not always . . .

In these words, Gouldner makes it clear that the title of his book is intended to convey two simple messages. The first is that the book is addressed to those who live 'for' sociology rather than 'off sociology'. The second is that the way in which the social sciences had developed in the twentieth century makes it necessary for those who live 'for sociology' to reassert their discipline's original Enlightenment aspiration to become a form of inquiry that would self-consciously advance emancipatory goals. *For Education* is intended to convey two similar messages. The first is that it speaks to and for all those educational theorists, educational researchers, teachers and teacher educators who live 'for education' rather than 'off education'. The second is that the moral, political and intellectual promise of educational theorizing and research depends on these people being prepared to devote their energies to conducting educational inquiries that can more genuinely express their educational aspirations and ideals.

It is a well known philosophical truism that one cannot think for oneself by oneself and the contents of this book are the product of an extended and sometimes tortuous argument that I have conducted with philosophers and educational theorists ranging from Plato, Kant and Hegel to Richard Peters, Hans Georg Gadamer and Thomas Kuhn. Fortunately for me, there is no one among this distinguished company who has had the opportunity of answering back. One person who has had this dubious privilege has been my close friend and colleague, Stephen Kemmis. It would be no exaggeration to say that the arguments and ideas expressed in this book would not – and perhaps could not – have developed in the way that they have if they had not been tested and revised through critical confrontation with Stephen's own very different arguments and ideas. It is entirely appropriate that he should have written the Prologue to this book and for this, and so much more, I owe him a special debt.

My debts to others are massive and too numerous to mention. I can only record my gratitude to all the friends, students and colleagues in Britain, Spain, Australia, Brazil and elsewhere who, by insisting that I engage with them in a systematic and critical discussion of my work, have played such a key part in making this book possible. Yet this book would still not have seen the light of day but for the diligence, conscientiousness and intelligent care shown by Ann Whorton in preparing and producing the final manuscript. For this I can do no more than express my gratitude and thanks. Gratitude and thanks of a very different kind are due to the four women in my life. It is to them that this book is dedicated.

ACKNOWLEDGEMENTS

Most of the chapters in this book are, to varying degrees, based on papers originally published elsewhere. I would like to thank the publishers of the following academic journals for their permission to reprint material from these papers here.

Chapter 1 'The gap between theory and practice', *Journal of Further and Higher Education*, 4(1), 60–69 (1980). 'Treating the symptoms, neglecting the cause: diagnosing the problem of theory and practice', *Journal of Further and Higher Education*, 6(2), 19–29 (1982).

Chapter 2 'Theories of theory and practice', *Journal of Philosophy of Education*, 20(2), 177–86 (1986).

Chapter 3 'Adopting an education philosophy', *Cambridge Journal of Education*, 4(2), 1–4 (1984).

Chapter 4 'What is an educational practice?', *Journal of Philosophy of Education*, 21(2), 163–75 (1987).

Chapter 5 'Can educational research be scientific?', *Journal of the Philosophy of Education*, 17(1), 35–45 (1983).

Chapter 6 'Philosophy, values and educational science', *Journal of Curriculum Studies*, 178(2), 119–32 (1985).

Chapter 7 'Action research: ten years on', *Journal of Curriculum Studies*, 21, 85–90 (1989).

Chapter 8   'Critical theory and educational studies', *Journal of Philosophy of Education*, 21(2), 287–95 (1987). 'The idea of an educational science', *Journal of Philosophy of Education*, 23(1), 29–37 (1989).

PROLOGUE: THEORIZING

EDUCATIONAL

PRACTICE

Stephen Kemmis

To the practising teacher, what could be more innocent, more transparent, more familiar than the notion of 'practice'? It is what we do. It is our work. It speaks for itself – or so we may think. But there is another point of view – that educational practice does not just 'speak for itself'. On this alternative view, educational practice is something made by people. Educational practice is a form of power – a dynamic force both for social continuity and for social change which, though shared with and constrained by others, rests largely in the hands of teachers. Through the power of educational practice, teachers play a vital role in changing the world we live in.

In his writings on the relationship between educational theory and practice, Wilfred Carr has challenged contemporary understandings of the nature of educational practice. Though not alone among contemporary educational philosophers, he has made at least three important contributions to our understanding of the relationship between educational theory and practice. One part of his contribution has been to show that the value, the significance and the meaning of practice is not self-disclosing: it is *constructed*. A second part of his contribution has been to revive and extend our understanding of the nature of reasoning about, in and through practice – on the one hand, recovering the Aristotelian view of *practical reasoning* and, on the other, enriching the Aristotelian view in the light of contemporary insights from critical social theory to reach towards a notion of *critical reasoning*. A third part of his contribution has been to show that these insights into the nature of practice and of practical and critical reasoning have significant consequences for educational research, revealing flaws and misconceptions in much of what now passes as educational research, and providing a basis upon which a more adequate form of educational research – *a critical science of education* – can be outlined.

These achievements seem almost modest when measured against the extravagant claims of other contemporary critical and 'postmodernist' educational and social theorists. There is a body of opinion in contemporary literary theory, history and social theory which suggests that the enduring questions of theory and practice have long been resolved. According to this view, the power of theory is always a form of power which reveals its connections to the entrenched interests of capital and the state, a form of power exercised 'over the heads' of teachers and, through teachers, over their students. On such a view, theory becomes no more than a manifestation of ideology, a form of legitimation of the interests of the state and capital – even, at worst, theory as no more than the velvet glove that masks the iron fist of state policy, which controls schooling in the interests of the state. While 'critical' in one sense, this view of theory is not critical enough for my liking. It fails to recognize the considerable resources that theory can provide, not only for unmasking the interests at work in contemporary education, but also for strengthening and sustaining education as a source of social movement as well as social order.[1]

According to the 'postmodern' view, the ghosts of positivism have long been laid to rest, and even the notion of 'critical theory' is so much to be taken for granted that it may already be regarded as *passé*. This impatience is, perhaps, as much an expression of the postmodern condition as a critical response to it; it is an impatience characteristic of a generation anxious to make its own mark on history. It betrays an enthusiasm for the new which risks other dangers – especially the danger that the hard work of detailed argument will be left behind in the quest for still further elaborations of the theme that knowledge is power, and that it develops in an unholy alliance with the powers that be, even where it means to challenge established power.

While the fashionable frontline of methodological debate has rushed forward, many educational theorists and researchers have comfortably sustained old (some 'modern' and some even 'premodern') and untenable views – like the notion of the 'gap' between theory and practice – which have bedevilled educational science for most of this century. The *avant-garde* may regard this old order of educational researchers as anachronistic, as dinosaurs, but the *ancien régime* still commands contemporary respect in learned journals and from senior administrators in education systems, and the old views are still widely reproduced through conventional courses on educational theory, research methodology and educational practice.

But it is not only the old guard of educational theorists and researchers that falls prey to the old assumptions and presuppositions. Too often, the *avant-garde* also relies on views about theory and practice which are no longer tenable. Indeed, some dangerous old assumptions have remained obstinately fixed in the shared contemporary consciousness of educational theorists and researchers, binding us in unacknowledged ways to the views of science characteristic of earlier times. Despite the apparent recognition among *avant-garde* theorists that practitioners are not mindless functionaries performing in accordance with the theories of others, or the apparent recognition that practice and theory develop reflexively and together, many researchers still proceed to study practice 'from the outside', believing that their insights, won in the intellectual struggle of the postgraduate seminar or the invitational international conference, will produce changes in the educational practice of teachers who attend neither. Wilfred Carr has helped to make it clear how we have been imprisoned in those old views, despite our sense of progress, and he continues to challenge some of the comfortable assumptions of contemporary theorists, like those about the role of educational research (and researchers) in providing guidance to practice (and practitioners). Not only does he assert that we must be as interested in the theories of 'practitioners' as we are in their practices, nor even that we must study the practices of 'theorists' just as closely as we study their theories; he also demonstrates how the work of educational practice and the work of theorizing must develop hand-in-hand.

This view has important implications for the organization and the micropolitics of education and educational research, suggesting that new forms of relationship must develop between the people we have conventionally come to regard as 'theorists' and those we conventionally regard as 'practitioners'. It implies the development of new collaborative forms of science which challenge the existing bureaucratic specialization of function and division of labour which structure schooling in the modern state.

Can practice be understood without reference to the self-understandings of actors?

As a psychologist trained in the behaviourist psychology of the 1960s, I was taught that, in order to understand the activity of human beings, it was necessary to look at action 'from the outside', as if it were controlled by a mechanism as mute, as hidden and as powerful as the mechanism that so harmoniously orders and so rigorously determines the movement of the planets and the stars. We behavioural scientists were heirs to the great tradition of Sir Isaac Newton (1642–1727). Finding the mathematical order which unified and explained the chaos of the world we could see and describe in an unselfconsciously masculinist image, we believed that by revealing nature's secrets, we would also learn to control her. The image of the mechanism was so powerful that the very task of behavioural science was driven by it. We were convinced that we knew what the 'truths' we sought looked like – they would be mathematical formulae, like those published in Newton's *Principia* of 1687, that described the secret mechanisms, springs and gears behind the surface of the material world. Despite the clamour, the struggle and the wildly proliferating diversity of the social and political life of the 1960s, behaviourist psychologists were trained to look at life like a silent movie (with ourselves responsible for adding the interspersed frames of text that gave a gloss to the action). Nowadays, we might think of it as rather like watching television soap operas with the sound turned down – as a game we play to make the unutterable ordinariness of most television programmes more interesting just because, without the words, they offer more scope for the imagination.

This view of human behaviour – as life with the sound turned down – is one that imagines that human beings only poorly understand the meanings and significance of their actions. It assumes that people rationalize their actions or that they deceive themselves (and others) about their actions much of the time. It implies that, no matter how 'rational' their actions may seem to the actors themselves, the scientists who study these actors are likely to be misled by knowing too much about people's own explanations of their behaviour. Once these assumptions were accepted, behavioural science could study human action as if it were best to know nothing at all of what people think.[2] From the perspective of behaviourist social science, this view of the objects of study and the methodologies appropriate for studying them has the very practical advantage (for the scientist at least) that it is left to the scientist to fill in the 'real' text: to interpret and explain the real meaning of social life. It was almost as if the scientist were an academic specialist given the task of interpreting and explaining the meaning of a medieval play to its cast of performers, though sometimes more significant roles were hinted at: we might not be just literary theorists, or even drama critics; perhaps we could become authors of texts for social and political life.

The preference for the view of human and social life as mechanical, as capable of being stripped of surface confusion and perplexity, is a product of a profound nineteenth-century faith in the power and possibilities of a certain kind of science – a kind of science able to 'see' beneath the surface of things to discover principles of order which account for the workings of the hidden mechanism beneath. The self-understandings of actors are regarded by this kind of science as extremely unreliable guides to the 'real' workings of their minds and lives; instead, it seeks hidden structures and motives. For some scientists, these are to be found in the structure and biochemistry of the nervous system; for others, they are to be found in habits, motives and 'laws of behaviour'. Put as its simplest, this form of science asserts that, in the end, people do not know what they are doing, and far less do they know why they are doing it. On this view of science, it is the task of the scientist to reveal the forces by which human action is determined, and later to make these discoveries available so that action can be more carefully controlled and directed.

Michel Foucault[3] and others have shown us how this nineteenth-century scientific tradition was an improvement on earlier forms of science. Those earlier forms frequently did no more than replace the surface mysteries of the nature and form of human life with other mysteries beneath. For example, in the seventeenth century astrology and the presumed propensities of particular star signs were used as a basis for botanical taxonomy and thus for explaining the diversity, nature and properties of plant life; in the eighteenth century, botanists began to seek orders of classification by reference to the structural features of plants themselves. In the late eighteenth and early nineteenth centuries, the idea of truth as representation had begun to take hold, and gave birth to the idea that explanation could be an extension of description. The diversity of plant forms would be explained when principles accounting for the diversity were discovered, that is, when the mechanisms producing the diversity were described. At one level, an explanation of continuity and diversity among plant forms was suggested through the experiments of Gregor Mendel (1822–84), which offered a theory of heredity – a theory which was explanatory because it pointed to the operation of genetic mechanisms governing the inheritance of dominant and recessive characters. At another level, an explanation of biological diversity and continuity was suggested through the work of Charles Darwin (1809–82), whose theory of evolution pointed to a mechanism of 'natural selection'.

From the nineteenth century onwards, natural and physical science was dominated by the search for hidden mechanisms whose existence and operation could explain the nature of things. It was a form of science which searched for the explanation of one order of describable phenomena (for example, the continuity and diversity of plant forms) through the description of a mechanism in another level of order (for example, the 'hidden' order of genetic characteristics).

This approach to science posed interesting problems for the human sciences. The late nineteenth century witnessed new developments in the theory of history, and the rise of anthropology, sociology and psychology. On the one hand, there were those who believed that the developing human sciences could be built on the foundations of hermeneutics in biblical exegesis, history and aesthetics; on the other hand, there were those who believed that the new sciences would need to follow the model of the natural and physical sciences. John Stuart Mill (1806–73) had defended the view that the social sciences could be built on the foundations of natural science, though admittedly as 'inexact' sciences (like a possible science of 'tidology' or the study of the tides) rather than as an 'exact' science (like physics); his argument was widely regarded as establishing a continuity of scientific principle between the social and natural sciences. Others were not so sure – they argued that there was a necessary discontinuity of principle between the social and natural sciences. In particular, in the late nineteenth and early twentieth centuries, a succession of German social theorists like Wilhelm Dilthey (1833–1911), Georg Simmel (1858–1918) and Max Weber (1864–1920) sought to extend and elaborate the idea of hermeneutic interpretation into an alternative epistemological basis for the social sciences. Weber, for example, defined sociology as

> a science which attempts the interpretive understanding of social action . . . In 'action' is included all human behaviour when and in so far as the acting individual attaches a subjective meaning to it. Action in this sense may be either overt, or purely inward or subjective; it may consist of positive intervention in a situation, or of deliberately refraining from such intervention or passively acquiescing in the situation. Action is social in so far as, by virtue of the subjective meaning attached to it by the acting individual (or individuals), it takes account of the behaviour of others and is thereby oriented in its course.[4]

Weber's stress on subjective meaning and action (as opposed to 'behaviour') suggested that a social science could not proceed without taking account of actors' own understandings of their action. Far from being 'noise' in the scientific system, self-understandings were regarded by Weber as an essential part of social action, and thus an essential part of the subject matter of sociology. To return to the television metaphor I used earlier: on Weber's view, turning the sound down would not strip practice of the irrelevant rationalizations and self-justifications of social actors; on the contrary, it would deprive the scientist of access to an important part of the subject matter of social science itself.

On the view of behaviourist psychology, then, practice could not be understood by reference to the self-understandings of actors, while to sociologists like Weber, it could not be understood without reference to actors' self-understandings. To reach an understanding of practice, it is necessary to find a way to resolve this issue.

One way to begin to do this is to think about practice as *constructed*. While we may be accustomed to thinking of practice as no more than 'activity', it can be shown that the meaning and significance of educational practice is socially, historically and politically constructed, and that it cannot be understood other than interpretively and critically. On this view, practice is not merely 'doing'. It is not a species of technical, instrumental action; it has meanings and significances which cannot be understood solely by observation of our actions. But its meaning and significance is not only subjective (a matter of the perspectives and self-understandings of practitioners), it is also something interpretively understood by others, and framed by history and tradition, as well as by ideology.

The meaning and significance of practice is constructed in at least four senses. First, we cannot adequately understand the meaning and significance of a practice without referring to the *intentions* of a practitioner. For example, when I signal that this student should speak in the classroom, it may be to find out what she knows about the topic; it may be to draw her waning attention back to the classroom discussion; it may be to have her speak on my behalf, telling the other students what I think they need to know; it may be to permit her to change the direction of the classroom discussion, taking us on to new topics. Unless the observer knows my purpose and my reading of the current state of the class, the meaning of my practice is unlikely to be plain.

Second, and in a broader sense, the meaning and significance of a practice is socially constructed. It is *interpreted* not only by the agent but also by others. The student I have singled out may feel concern, pride, shame or enthusiasm, depending on her interpretation of my actions. And her classmates also interpret the meaning and significance of my action against their own particular, idiosyncratic frames of reference.

Third, and in a still broader sense, the meaning and significance of a practice is *historically constructed*. At one level, it must be interpreted against the background of the history of this situation. What is the history of my relationship with this student: is she a leader in class discussion, a model for others, an antagonist opposing my intentions for the class? This particular action is located in a stream of actions of which we, and the others in our class and our school, are all parts.

At another level, my actions have meaning and significance by reference to deeper traditions of educational practice, etched out over years, decades, perhaps even centuries. Am I striving to fulfil child-centred, liberal-progressive ideals? Am I transmitting skills or the high culture of our society in a more classical humanist way? Or am I striving to create democratic conditions of classroom discourse in keeping with more critical, perhaps even radical, ideals? To understand my practice profoundly, I must also make reference to the history of my situation and the educational traditions which give it a deeper form and structure.

Fourth, the meaning and significance of a practice is *politically constructed*. My classroom creates a micro-politics in which what happens may be shaped by domination and subjugation, or perhaps by open and democratic discourse and decision making. Some in the class have a greater influence over what happens, and some less; some have a greater share in the fruits of our labours, some less. And beyond these micro-politics, the practice of the classroom is also shaped by social, material and historical factors beyond the control of anyone in the room – by class relations, gender relations, language and cultural factors, and the like. In turn, the practice of the classroom creates some possibilities for the future lives of my students (and myself) and limits other possibilities. Yet the classroom is not a mirror of the political, cultural and economic structures of the wider society, nor is it a model of what the world outside should be. Without reference to these broader structures and their ideological character, we lack a critical understanding of the meaning and significance of educational practice.

Understanding and controlling practice: a task for God, for humankind, for capital or the modern state?

While the mechanistic view of science which developed in the nineteenth century reached forward into the social science of the twentieth century, it may also be argued that it reached back into far older traditions of European thought, retaining interesting affinities with theological traditions, though allowing the scientist to usurp the privileged place in the universe previously occupied by God. At least since the rise of what we think of as the emergence of science in the work of Roger Bacon (*c.*1214–94), there has been an argument about whether only God could understand the workings of the universe (including the workings of history, human societies and humankind), or whether it was part of the task of humankind to decipher God's secrets and to learn more about His grand design for the world through the evidence of His creation. Umberto Eco's wonderful novel *The Name of the Rose*[5] invites us to consider the terrifying prospect faced by humankind on the brink of this new form of science: the prospect that humankind would lose its fear of the awe of God's mystery, its hope in His redemptive power, its fear of His retributive justice and its obedience to His will once it possessed sufficient knowledge to make decisions and control events without reference to the authority of His word (as faithfully interpreted, not extended, by His servants the monks).

The idea of a 'positivist' science was developed in the nineteenth century by Auguste Comte (1798–1857). By use of the term 'positive', he intended to convey an opposition to any metaphysical or theoretical claims that some kind of non-sensorily apprehended experience could form the basis of valid knowledge. This was a radical and progressive claim for the time, promising both liberation from dogmatic theological certainties and improvement in the power of people over their circumstances through the application of 'positive' knowledge to their practical problems. It was an expression of the Enlightenment hope that human knowledge, not just knowledge of God, could free humankind from suffering and domination, and that hopes for humankind could be redeemed here on earth, whether or not in heaven.

By this time, humankind had begun to think very differently about knowledge. It had become part of the task of humankind to learn God's order of and for the world by studying nature – and human nature – more deeply. Perhaps investigating the fruit of the Tree of Knowledge could provide maps for getting back into Eden, since eating the fruit had once led to banishment from Eden and estrangement from God. Increasingly, humankind was becoming a kind of repository and source of knowledge about the world, and, in this way, becoming still more like the God in whose image human beings had been created. But a new dimension of God-like-ness had also been introduced. With the rise of Scientific Man (and, yes, the image of the scientist was tellingly stereotyped as masculine in those times), humankind would become God-like in its capacity to reorder the world on more rational principles. This rationalistic faith was partly based on ideas about what constituted an ordered economy; it also reflected progressive democratic ideals of European (and North American) nation states of the nineteenth century. What was different in the new order was that while God had always 'moved in mysterious ways his wonders to perform', Scientific Man could put himself at the disposal of the great historical forces of progress and democracy, to intervene explicitly and overtly in the workings of human history.

The philosopher Barry Hindess sees this view of social science as based on 'a rationalistic theory of action' (as distinct from a rationalist epistemology). He writes:

> Rationalist epistemology conceives of the world as a rational order in the sense that its parts and the relations between them conform to concepts and the relations between them, the concept giving the essence of real. Where rationalist epistemology presupposes an *a priori* correspondence, a pre-given harmony, between ideas and the world, the rationalist conception of action postulates a mechanism of the realisation of ideas. For example, in Weber's conception of action as 'oriented in its course' by meanings, the relation between action and meaning is one of coherence and logical consistency: the action realises the logical consequences of its meaning. Is it necessary to point out the theological affinities of this conception of action? While theology postulates God as the mechanism *par excellence* of the realisation of the world, the rationalist conception of !action conceives of a lesser but not essentially dissimilar mechanism.[6]

But it was not just 'the scientist' who would reorder the world. Science had already proved its worth in the natural and physical sciences by ordering and developing knowledge which assisted the development of new technologies, especially the technologies required for industrial development. The alliance of science with the interests of the increasingly powerful industrialists of the nineteenth century suggested that other alliances might be possible: alliances with social reformers and even with the established interests of the state. While few scientists thought of themselves as being like Plato's philosopher-kings, they were willing to see themselves as the servants of the powerful, contributing to the development of a better, more rational world. In a variety of fields of social welfare and education, scientists contributed enthusiastically to the developing professionalization of science as a means for institutionalizing their own roles in the operation of the modern state. As the twentieth century wore on, the rise of the meritocracy in Western democratic states began to be eclipsed by the ascendance of a technocracy.

In the first three decades of the twentieth century, an increasingly sharp set of distinctions began to emerge between social scientists, the people social scientists study, and the social policy-makers the scientists serve. This set of distinctions provided the basis for a division of labour: social scientists began to distinguish themselves, on the one hand, from 'the general public' (which was increasingly regarded as an object of study) and, on the other, from the representatives of the state (increasingly regarded as the sponsors and legitimate users of scientific knowledge, and of the power made possible through its application). In this period, social scientists began to seek ways to increase their bargaining power in their relations with governments and policy-makers through asserting rights of academic freedom and professional responsibility. In a democratic society, this set of relations raises nice questions about whose interests science serves.

Despite the intentions of nineteenth-century scientists to liberate humankind from religious dogma, the emerging science and social science of the late nineteenth and early twentieth centuries had (as has been noted) an affinity with those earlier theological views: a rationalistic theory of action in which actions were seen as the expression and realization of ideas. Knowledge was increasingly seen as a source of power – indeed, as Foucault points out, the division of labour between the scientists (whose task it is to know), the representatives of the state (whose task it is to make decisions) and the general public (the object of knowledge and decisions) is a relationship of power (or 'power/knowledge').

The rationalistic theory of action privileges theory over practice in the notion that theory is a guide for practice. It predicates practice on theory, obscuring the ways in which theory is itself predicated on practice. On the one side, it permits a power relationship to arise in which those whose tasks are theorizing may be seen as hierarchically and managerially superordinate to those whose tasks are practice; on the other side, it demeans (and deskills) practice and practitioners as sources of ideas (theory). The rationalistic theory of action remains deeply embedded in the common conception of what it means to be an educational theorist or researcher (or academic, or scientist) as distinct from what it means to be a practitioner. The one is expected to be articulate, a source of ideas about how the work of education should be done in order to be effective; the other is expected to learn the hard-won lessons of educational science and to apply them in practice (following orders?). This view has the contradictory implication that it regards practitioners as poorly informed about practice even though they know it 'from the inside', while regarding theorists as well informed about practice even though they are removed from it by the division of labour.

The relationship between theory and practice in educational science: technical, practical or critical?

It is perhaps characteristic of the progress of social and educational science that, for almost the whole of this century, such debates over epistemological and methodological questions (like 'what is the nature of humankind or society?' and 'how should education be studied?') have remained unresolved – no strong agreements emerged on the 'true', essential nature of social or educational science, despite the virtual methodological hegemony of positivism, empiricism and behaviourism in educational psychology from the 1930s to the 1960s. Instead, educational research and research method followed a variety of disciplinary traditions and a variety of methods. Indeed, by mid-century, some educational theorists had begun to make a virtue of this eclecticism, following the argument that knowledge about education was not distinctive (in the way that knowledge in certain disciplines could be), and that educational knowledge was therefore obliged to develop on the coat-tails of knowledge in such 'foundational' disciplines as psychology, sociology, history and philosophy. With the rise of the 'foundations' movement[7] in the USA and the 'educational theory' movement[8] in the UK, education began to be regarded as an 'applied science', or as a derivative field from which it was necessary to appeal to competing disciplines and traditions of inquiry thought to be relevant to educational problems. It was tantamount to saying that education was *only* a practical field, and that theoretical knowledge about it was always theoretical knowledge about *something else* (for example, the psychology of learning or the sociology of schools).

Far from resolving the disputes between the disciplines, one might almost say that the new eclecticism of the 'foundations' movement (in the USA) and the 'educational theory' movement (in the UK) created platforms for reviving and structuring the debate about the nature and objects of educational science and educational theory. Both the 'foundations' and 'educational theory' settlements were galling to teachers and teachers of educational studies. Not only did they suggest that practitioners of education studies would always have a kind of derivative status *vis-à-vis* the practitioners of other fields of inquiry, they also conceded that education was without distinctive theoretical content (a particularly paradoxical achievement for an 'educational theory' movement). In conceding that the study of education was not and could not be a 'discipline' in its own right, this settlement threatened to deprive education and educationists of a distinctive sense of method. At this point the debate took a new turn, particularly (in the USA) through the work of Joseph Schwab[9] (who had himself been an exponent of the disciplines, and had written about the conditions which gave fields of inquiry their distinctiveness[10]). Schwab's contribution was significant in creating a rallying point for reaction against the 'applied science' view of curriculum by drawing on the work of the neo-Aristotelian philosopher Richard McKeon[11] to revive interest in different modes of reasoning. In doing so, Schwab recovered some of the meta-theoretical presuppositions of contemporary educational science.

In *The Nicomachean Ethics*, Aristotle[12] had distinguished technical, practical and (what we might call) scientific reasoning. Technical (instrumental, means–ends) reasoning presupposes given ends and, following known rules, uses given materials and means to achieve these ends. Examples of this 'making' action are the making of a pot or a poem; in education, examples would be the use of research findings on the effects of questions interpolated in text when preparing a textbook, or following rules of reinforcement in determining principles of reward and punishment in a classroom. At the level of an education system, the use of programme planning and budgeting systems and the use of performance indicator systems as accountability devices are examples of technical reason at work.

Practical reasoning, by contrast, does not assume known ends or given means, and does not follow imposed rules of method; instead, it is the form of reasoning appropriate in social, political and other situations in which wise persons, drawing on experience, reason about how to act truly and rightly in given historical circumstances (with both ends and means being problematic).[13] While technical reason expresses itself in 'making' action, practical reason expresses itself in 'doing' action. Classical examples of practical reasoning are those of the politician deciding on a course of action appropriate for particular social and political demands and circumstances, or the military commander forced to decide whether to fight on or withdraw in the face of possible defeat. An educational example would be that of a teacher deciding whether to discipline a misbehaving student or to treat the occasion of the misbehaviour as an educational opportunity for discussing the nature and consequences of this kind of misbehaviour. At the level of an education system, the decision of senior policy-makers about whether to introduce a system of accountability based on performance indicators could well be reached on the basis of practical reasoning (weighing up both ends and means and deciding whether the game is worth the candle).

According to Aristotle, 'scientific' reasoning (*theoria*) is the pursuit of purely intellectual questions – examples might include analytic philosophy or pure mathematics – a mode of reasoning which informs the contemporary idea of 'pure' (as opposed to 'applied') science.

Schwab's particular contribution in 'The practical' was in distinguishing the practical mode of reasoning required for resolving curriculum questions from the technical mode of reasoning used in applying theoretical knowledge. On the basis of a scathing analysis of the limitations and 'incompetences' of the 'theoretic', he put a strong case for the arts of 'practical deliberation' (as well as the 'eclectic' and the 'quasi-practical') in resolving the educational questions which confront educators in their day-to-day lives.

At about the same time, but from an entirely different intellectual tradition, the German philosopher of social science Jürgen Habermas was also drawing on Aristotle to unmask the meta-theoretical presuppositions of contemporary social science. In his theory of knowledge-constitutive interests,[14] Habermas returned to Aristotle's notions of modes of reasoning (at the same time reinterpreting Aristotle's notion of *theoria*) in developing a critique of the nature and functions of social science.

Habermas's argument is that different forms of science not only employ different modes of reasoning, but also (in a materialist and neo-Marxist turn of argument) serve different kinds of interests through creating or constituting knowledge – hence the term 'knowledge-constitutive' interests. According to Habermas, empirical-analytic science (in political science, sociology, anthropology etc.) employed the kind of technical reasoning identified by Aristotle. Recognizing its instrumental, means–ends character, he described this form of science as guided by a *technical* interest. The hermeneutic sciences (including much history and aesthetic criticism, and some forms of psychology, sociology and anthropology), by contrast, employed what Aristotle described as practical modes of reasoning; hence, Habermas described them as guided by a *practical* knowledge-constitutive interest – an interest in guiding, informing and educating readers by interpreting the world and our understandings of it, distilling experience and providing examples of the historical consequences of acting one way or another (rightly or wrongly) under different historical circumstances.

Following the critical theory tradition of the Frankfurt School,[15] however, Habermas reconstructed Aristotle's notion of *theoria* away from the notion of 'pure' science towards a more materialist grounding in the actions and practices of social scientists (and others, including social policy-makers and social activists) who, at their best, work in the interests of rationality, justice and freedom. He described this as an *emancipatory* interest. Habermas's early works *Knowledge and Human Interests* and *Theory and Practice* not only outline the character of an emancipatory social science by drawing on the critical theory tradition of the Frankfurt School, but also promise the development of a *critical social science* in which the values of justice and freedom (interpreted in participatory democratic terms) are as indispensable to the character of scientific work as the values of truth and rationality. Indeed, in his theory of communicative competence and the 'ideal speech situation'[16] (later developed in his *The Theory of Communicative Action, Volumes 1 and 2*), he aimed to show how the conditions for establishing truth and rationality were fundamentally connected to the conditions for free, democratic communication and action.

The critical social science of Habermas is not merely a theory of action of the psychological or sociological kind, aiming to demonstrate connections between thought and action of individuals, or even in professional and other groups (as may be found in the notion of the 'reflective practitioner' developed by Donald Schon[17]). A critical social science is a species of social theory which, in separate but related ways, aims at

- ideology critique (criticism of the nature and social relations of production, reproduction and social transformation, including the circumstances and consciousness of people as individuals, members of groups and bearers of culture);

- the organization of enlightenment in social groups and societies (including some kinds of educational processes); and
- the organization of social and political action to improve the world (guided by a dialectical notion of rationality, and a communitarian, egalitarian notion of justice and freedom).

Thus understood, a critical social or educational science is not just a means to individual enlightenment (as might be advocated in some liberal views of social or educational science), but a mode of collective social action profoundly connected to emancipatory ideals of rationality, justice and freedom. On this view, the continuing development of educational theory and practice is a matter for educational practitioners (working with others), not just for educational theorists and researchers outside schools.

Teachers' reflections, private knowledge and public theory: implications for a science of education

For most teachers, including teachers of education studies, theorizing about education is something that occurs away from practice. It happens at sites and times other than the sites and times of practice itself. Our images of the sites of theorizing are ones involving books and armchairs, or desks and blank sheets of paper; our expectation about the time for theorizing is that it happens outside the hurly-burly of the teaching day, perhaps in the restorative peace of evening or in the crystal clarity of morning (some people's mornings, anyway). We nevertheless think about these sites and times of theorizing as significant for practice. Retrospectively, they permit interpretation of practical puzzlements; prospectively, they promise guidance, perhaps even prescriptions for practice.

These images of theorizing focus on the relationship between *thought and action*: the ways in which the conduct of practitioners is mediated by ideas. There is a growing literature of reflection which concerns itself with just this relationship between thought and action, recently given new impetus by Donald Schon's notion of the 'reflective practitioner'.[18] If theory and theorizing are understood in terms of reflection, they seem to refer to aspects of cognitive functioning, including the relationship of ideas to action: how reflection expresses itself in the life and work of the practitioner. On this basis, we might speak of every practitioner as being guided by theory, meaning no more by this than that the practitioner has ideas. But it can be shown that this is an insufficient basis for asserting that a practitioner has a theory.

The thought-and-action view of the relationship between theory and practice is individualistic. In addition (as argued earlier), it presupposes a one-sided, rather rationalistic[19] view of theorizing, emphasizing the power of ideas to guide or even direct action, rather than the way action and the circumstances of action also shape our ideas, pre-forming and limiting both our understandings of the actual circumstances in which we find ourselves and our notions of what is possible. This narrower, frequently individualistic and rationalistic view of the relationship between theory and practice (which treats it in terms of thought and action) should be distinguished from a broader conception of the relationship between theory and practice which treats both in terms of *public processes*.

One way to begin to address the relationship between theory and practice as a public process is to consider theory and practice in terms of social relationships and social structures. One might begin by seeing these social relationships in terms of *roles*. For most of us, it is not just that the sites and times of theorizing (or should we now say 'reflection'?) are separated from sites and times of practice; as argued earlier, theorizing and practising are also separated in the larger social framework by the division of labour and differentiation of function in the institutional structures of contemporary schooling. There are people whose primary tasks are understood to be theorizing (educational theorists, for example), and others (teachers) whose primary tasks are understood to be practice. True, the 'official' theorists may also be practitioners for some of their time, and the 'official' practitioners may also sometimes be theorists, but the common conception is that the primary responsibilities of each are distinctive. The theorist is seen as making a contribution to education from the library, the laboratory, the desk or the podium, the practitioner in face-to-face interaction with students. It is as if, in the overall division of labour of schooling, we had our own version of the distinction between mental and manual labour, or white- and blue-collar workers; as if, in the broad institutional structure of schooling, we had our own distinctions between the business office and the mineshaft or factory floor.

The analysis of theory and practice in terms of roles soon becomes muddied, however, when we think about the complex of relationships between (so-called) theorists' theories and practices and (so-called) practitioners' theories and practices. We need to be clear about exactly what (and whose) practices and what (and whose) theories are being considered at any time. As already suggested, people do not stay neatly in role: at times, setting aside the role of practitioner of theorizing, the educational theorist is a practitioner of education (a teacher); at times the teacher (as educational practitioner) is a theorist. And there are further complexities: it may be that theorists' theories are usually aimed at explaining or interpreting practitioners' practices, or even at explaining or interpreting practitioners' theories; in general, however, educational theorists have given less attention to explaining their own theories of their own educational (or teaching) practices. Moreover, despite the vast (and idealized) literature of research methodology, there is also a reluctance among educational theorists to theorize their practice of theorizing as a lived experience or as a form of work.[20] Though related, the different, institutionally separated practices of educational theorizing and teaching may need different theories to explain, interpret or justify them.

Such an analysis, beginning from roles, can help us to clarify just what practices are being theorized, when and by whom. From this beginning, we can make a more robust analysis of the processes of theorizing and practising. When we are clear about just what practices (or what theories) are the focus of our analysis, we discover that theory and practice cannot be separated. As Wilfred Carr and I argued in *Becoming Critical*,[21] it is by being theorized that practices have meaning (as practices of a certain kind), and it is by being practised that theories have historical, social and material significance. Theory is not just words, and practice is not mute behaviour; theory and practice are mutually constitutive aspects of one another. On this view, there can be no 'gap' between theory and practice, only greater and lesser degrees of mismatch, elision and illusion in the relationship between them. We can only identify these mismatches, elisions and illusions by examining how our theories and practices interrelate. In general, practices of theorizing educational practice are related *through practices*. They are related through human and social activities which understand themselves to be related to theory; for example, the *application* of theory, or the *decision* to act in a certain way on the basis of a certain perspective, or, at their best, through public processes – practices – of *critical reflection and self-reflection*.[22]

The relationship between theory and practice, on a broad view, must be understood in terms of the public sphere rather than the private (the mediation of thought and action in the life and work of an individual). In this spirit, Lawrence Stenhouse defined research as a public activity: 'Research is systematic enquiry made public. It is made public for criticism and utilization within a particular research tradition.'[23]

At least potentially, knowledge becomes theory by being tested, justified and sustained through debate in a public sphere. The testing and justifying of new ideas and insights is a process of theorizing which establishes agreements and disagreements of the new knowledge with what others know; by its reconciliation with what others have already contributed to a common stock of knowledge, it is given a place in the public realm of theory. Such theoretical knowledge bears a different kind of relationship to action from private knowledge. Theoretical knowledge is mediated not only through the minds of individuals but also through public processes in which actions come to be understood as practices, as activities of a certain type, whose meaning and significance is shared among groups of people, perhaps whole communities. As Alasdair MacIntyre[24] has argued, practices are judged by reference to publicly shared criteria and traditions; by reference to the lives, virtues and excellences of practitioners as the bearers of these traditions; and by reference to the work of institutions created in order to nurture and sustain these activities and the values, virtues and excellences they embody and express.

On the broader view, then, the mediation of theory and practice is a public process. It relates a common stock of theoretical ideas, understood in the framework of traditions of thought, to theorized activities, regulated as practices (frequently within the structured framework of institutions). Exploring the mediation of theory and practice is, on this view, a public task, realized through social processes of research and evaluation, though of course they also have a private face. Individuals consider theoretical ideas and their implications for practice, drawing private conclusions about what to do in given circumstances, no doubt, but they do so with a conscious awareness that both theory and practice are open to judgement by others, in relation to publicly accessible criteria and in the light of circumstances. At such times, individuals place themselves under the authority of traditions and under the judgement of history, and perhaps (more immediately and more concretely) under the auspices of institutions. Their work is no longer to be understood as private activity, but rather as the embodiment and realization of educational ideals, values and traditions of which they and others (some close by, and some very distant from us) are bearers, and to which they are contemporary contributors. In short, individuals may reflect and act privately on their understandings of theory and practice, but the development of theory and practice depends on the conscious participation of individuals in a public process – in one form or another, in research as Stenhouse defined it. The development of theory and practice requires our participation as individuals, but at the same time makes us more than individuals – it makes us the bearers of traditions, responsible with others for continuing the debates through which the traditions may be defended and strengthened, or through which they may properly be laid to rest.[25]

This view of the relationship between theory and practice involves a notion of politics – the politics of debate. For MacIntyre, the politics is liberal individualism, a debate in which individuals advance, defend, attack and counterattack arguments guided by different views of rationality and practical reasoning, whose roots he traces back to Athens in the fifth and fourth centuries BC. An alternative to MacIntyre's view[26] is that of Habermas, whose view is based on a politics of discussion in which the conditions for rational discussion are those of democratic participation in discourse. Habermas describes the 'ideal speech situation' – note that he is describing an *ideal* speech situation, not the conditions of usual discourse in groups – necessary for a rational consensus:

> the design of an ideal speech situation is necessarily implied in the structure of potential speech, since all speech, even intentional deception, is oriented towards the idea of truth . . . In so far as we master the means for the construction of the ideal speech situation, we conceive the ideas of truth, freedom and justice.[27]

What is common to the different accounts of the politics of debate given by MacIntyre and Habermas is a sense that rationality does involve a politics – and that it is a public process of reclaiming and extending not merely meanings (for individuals) but also agreements between people reached on the basis of (public) argument. While MacIntyre emphasizes the location of debate in history and traditions, Habermas emphasises the location of debate in the social processes of real groups striving for consensus. And in elaborating the politics of the process of debate, Habermas begins to identify those practices which constitute rationality in debate: the raising, challenging and redeeming of 'validity claims' which are, he argues, presupposed by all utterances. These are the implicit claims that what is spoken is (a) comprehensible, (b) true, (c) right or appropriate in a given situation and (d) truthfully or sincerely stated. In discourse (a level of debate about what is being communicated), speakers explore the validity claims presupposed in their communication with one another. Thomas McCarthy outlines the kinds of practices of communication characteristic of Habermas's ideal speech situation, drawing attention to the key contention that the conditions for truth telling are also the conditions for democratic discussion:

> The very act of participating in the discourse, of attempting discursively to come to an agreement about the truth of a problematic statement or the correctness of a problematic norm, carries with it the presupposition that a genuine agreement is possible. If we did not suppose that a justified consensus were possible and could in some way be distinguished from a false consensus, then the very meaning of discourse, indeed of speech, would be called into question. In attempting to come to a 'rational' decision about such matters, we must suppose that the outcome of our discussion will be the result simply of the force of the better argument, and not of accidental or systematic constraints on discussion. Habermas's thesis is that the structure [of communication] is free from constraint only when for all participants there is a symmetrical distribution of chances to select and employ speech acts, when there is an effective equality of chances to assume dialogue roles. In particular, all participants must have the same chance to initiate or perpetuate discourse, to put forward, to call into question, and give reasons for and against statements, interpretations, explanations and justifications. Furthermore, they must have the same chance to express attitudes, feelings, intentions and the like, and to command, to oppose, to permit, and to forbid, etc. In other words, the conditions of the ideal speech situation must ensure discussion which is free from all constraints of domination. Thus, the conditions for ideal discourse are connected with conditions for an ideal form of life; they include linguistic conceptualizations of the traditional ideas of freedom and justice. 'Truth', therefore, cannot be analyzed independently of 'freedom' and 'justice'.[28]

On this argument, the relationship of theory to practice is not merely a cognitive function, nor merely a matter of social roles or relationships; theorizing, too, is a public process and a social practice. Who participates in this public process, this social practice, is crucial not only in terms of whose interests are served by educational theorizing, but also in terms of what the substance of educational theorizing will be – what educational theorizing will be about. What Wilfred Carr shows in this book is that if it is to be about the questions that concern and puzzle educational practitioners, then an educational science will require the participation of practitioners in educational theorizing as a part of the process of improving educational practice.

INTRODUCTION: BECOMING
AN EDUCATIONAL
PHILOSOPHER

> Whatever happens, every individual is a child of his own
> time; so philosophy too is its own time apprehended in
> thought. It is just as absurd to fancy that a philosophy can
> transcend its temporal world as it is to fancy that an
> individual can overleap his own age.[1]

A few years ago, while clearing out some boxes from my mother's attic, I came
across an old school history textbook. I turned to the flyleaf and read what I
had written there.

> Wilfred Carr
> 97 Beresford Street
> Moss Side
> Manchester
> Lancashire
> England
> Great Britain
> United Kingdom
> Europe
> The World
> The Solar System
> The Universe

This kind of primitive cosmology was not uncommon in 1957 and it is probably
still a popular means for children to secure themselves against their initial lack of
placement by locating themselves in a reality that is familiar and knowable. The

discovery of this childhood inscription simply reminded me of myself as a typical thirteen-year-old schoolboy trying to find himself in a world that he was still experiencing as ambiguous, fragmentary and incomprehensible.

But the unearthing of this extended address also provided me with a vivid illustration of a couple of philosophical insights concerning some similarities between the way we grasp the meaning of concepts and the way we understand ourselves. One of these is captured by the notion of *embeddedness*: the insight that it is impossible to understand either our concepts or ourselves without also understanding something of the social and cultural contexts in which each is embedded. Just as I can only grasp the meaning of a concept by clarifying the role it plays in constituting a particular form of social life, so I can only gain an adequate sense of who and what I am, by reference to the range of social communities in which my self-identity has been formed. It is no doubt for this reason that my childhood exercise in self-understanding involved listing my membership of precisely those forms of community – the street, the neighbourhood, the city, the region, the nation state – to which I belonged.

Another insight into the relationship between conceptual understanding and self-understanding invoked by my childhood discovery concerns the relationship between *continuity and change*: the realization that, in the course of the passage of time, both the meaning of our concepts and our understanding of ourselves may change and become something other than they once were. But in neither of these cases is the process of change so complete as to allow either our understanding of a concept or our sense of who we are to become totally detached from their historical roots. So although a concept – such as the concept of 'philosophy' or the concept of 'education' – may now mean something very different to what it meant to past generations, it nevertheless always retains enough of its original meaning to enable us to recognise it as a concept of one and the same thing. Similarly, although the physical, intellectual and cultural transformations occurring in the subsequent life of the child who wrote this extended address now make it virtually impossible to perceive any connection between him and me, it nevertheless remains the case that he and I are nothing other than two episodes in the continuous and unbroken historical narrative that constitutes a single and unified human life. The biography of an individual, like the genealogy of a concept, is always a story about unity through diversity, continuity through change.

It was no doubt my idle reflections about these similarities that drew my interest towards the actual contents of my listing. I was born in the great city of Manchester, the home of radical liberalism and the cradle of the Industrial Revolution. I still speak with that Mancunian accent which Londoners and others from the south-east of England continue to hear as a deformed version of Received Standard Pronunciation that is inappropriate for serious intelligent talk. The part of Manchester where I lived, Moss Side, is now a notorious slum but during my childhood it was a respectable working class area that gave no sign of its coming seediness. 97 Beresford Street was a typical 'two-up-two-down' set in the middle of one of the endless rows of neat, clean terraced houses. It was a short distance from the house where David Lloyd George was born and even nearer to the house where the novelist Anthony Burgess spent the childhood he vividly describes in the first volume of his autobiography *Little Wilson and Big God*.[2]

Like Burgess I was a cradle Catholic of Irish blood and so, like him, I was sent to Bishop Bilsborrow Memorial School where, with considerable violence, the nuns from the Loreto convent taught me the Catholic gospel of love. They also taught me some secular things: to read and write and rattle off my tables. Because I learned these things better than most I was able to continue emulating Anthony Burgess by transferring to the Xaverian College, a Catholic grammar school whose namesake – Saint Francis Xavier – had been a Spanish pillar of the counter reformation and one of the seven co-founders of the Jesuits. With the help of a few lay teachers, the Xaverian Brothers who ran the school taught me Latin, English grammar, history and the other academic subjects of the traditional English grammar school curriculum. And, with the help of a few Jesuits, they saw to it that I continued to absorb the great grim doctrines of Catholicism.

I left school when I was sixteen and within a couple of years I had cut the cord with Mother Church. But, like any other mother, Catholicism is something you are stuck with forever and I was left with the intellectual attitudes and dispositions that are endemic to the Catholic way of thinking but easily withstand separation from their theological origins: a strong sense of history and tradition, a contempt for illogicality in all its forms and a deep-rooted suspicion of science and scientific knowledge. My loss of faith was also accompanied by something else which is familiar to the lapsed Catholic: a desire to somehow make good this 'loss' by finding substitute answers to the questions to which Catholicism had previously provided answers. It is a desire that is more emotional than intellectual and, in my case, found expression in a compulsive urge to ask awkward questions combined with a stubborn refusal to be fobbed off with authoritative answers offered by 'experts'. Many years later I was able to understand this compulsion as a manifestation of what another erstwhile Catholic – Terry Eagleton – called 'the demand to theorize'. Eagleton explains its origins in the following words.

> Children make the best theorists, since they have not yet been educated into accepting our routine social practices as 'natural', and so insist on posing to those practices the most embarrassingly general and fundamental questions, regarding them with a wondering estrangement which we adults have long forgotten. Since they do not yet grasp our social practices as inevitable, they do not see why we might not do things entirely differently. 'Where does capitalism come from Mummy?' is thus the prototypical theoretical question, one which usually receives what one might term a Wittgensteinian reply: 'This is just the way we do things dear'. It is those children who remain discontent with this shabby parental response who tend to grow up to be emancipatory theorists, unable to conquer their amazement at what everyone else seems to take for granted.[3]

Fourteen years after leaving school and twelve years after leaving the Catholic Church the inability to curb my childish predilection for asking 'the most embarrassingly general and fundamental questions' had taken me back into the world of education, first as a history teacher, then as a philosophy student and finally as a university lecturer in the philosophy of education at the University College of North Wales. When, in 1974, I was appointed to this post, I was confident that I had found an environment in which I could systematically pursue the kind of questions that my Catholic upbringing had left me prone to ask. After all, what had united educational philosophers from Plato onwards was their shared conviction that the underlying impulse to philosophize about education was a passionate concern for fundamental questions about the aims and purposes of human life and it was to their answers to these questions that they turned to justify the educational theories they advocated. Even those educational philosophers like John Dewey – whose style of thought was anti-theological and entirely secular – were at home with these 'big' issues.

But in 1974 educational philosophers had long since come to regard the once familiar and valid concern for these fundamental issues as a source of embarrassment. Indeed, anybody naive enough to expect philosophers of education to provide *a* philosophy of education was told that

> Professional philosophers are embarrassed by such expectations . . . Few . . . would now think it their function to provide such high level directives for education . . . indeed one of their main preoccupations has been to lay bare such aristocratic pronouncements.[4]

This reluctance to provide *a* philosophy of education was encouraged by two related claims that, at the time, received widespread support. One was the 'end of ideology' thesis as propounded by Daniel Bell: the claim that, in the intellectual landscape of Western societies, ideologically inspired proposals for a radical transformation of the social order were out of place.[5] The other was the claim that the attempts of past philosophers to construct general social political or educational philosophies should now be regarded as old-fashioned failures to keep up with the scientific times. When combined, these two claims were sufficient to persuade educational philosophers to abandon the study of educational philosophies – with their unsatisfactory mixture of ideological commitment, value judgements and empirical assertion – and to redefine their discipline in a non-ideological and more academically respectable way.

It was against this background that the philosophy of education came to be redefined as a method of inquiry which would transform the discipline from an endless battleground for competing educational ideologies into a respectable value-neutral academic pursuit. Though the definitions of this 'method' were various and often inadequate (linguistic philosophy, ordinary language philosophy, conceptual analysis) they nevertheless pointed to an essential truth: that the task of the philosophy of education was to elucidate the meanings of basic educational concepts by analysing the logical conditions governing the terms used to express them. By embracing this method, the philosophy of education could present itself as a legitimate branch of academic philosophy that was no longer contaminated by ideological conflict but had matured into a genuine and respectable academic discipline. Paul Hirst made the point in the following words.

> Philosophy . . . is above all concerned with clarification of the concepts and propositions through which our experiences and activities are intelligible – it is interested in answering questions about the meaning of terms and expressions . . . As I regard it, philosophy . . . is not the pursuit of moral knowledge . . . it is rather . . . primarily an analytical pursuit . . . Philosophy, as I see it, is a second order area of knowledge . . . Philosophical questions, are not about say, particular facts or moral judgements but about what we mean by facts, what we mean by moral judgements.[6]

Since its inception, the view that philosophy is concerned with the 'clarification of concepts' has been so severely criticized that its claim to define the nature and scope of philosophy were (with the notable exception of the philosophy of education) never taken very seriously. Without going into detail, most of these criticisms stemmed from a persistent failure to recognize that the concepts we use in ordinary language have histories and sustain inherited common-sense ways of thinking and acting that are impregnated with the religious myths and ideological prejudices of the past.[7] Under the misapprehension that thought is enslaved by language, conceptual analysis resolutely refused to see the point of questioning the adequacy of established concepts and so was quite incapable of exposing and criticizing the confusions and contradictions they contained. Even in 1974, it seemed obvious to me that, by adopting this method, the philosophy of education was simply depriving itself of all creative or critical purpose and denying itself the opportunity for radical educational thinking of any kind.

But at that time, my main worries about this kind of philosophy of education reflected a personal rather than a purely intellectual concern. In the 1970s the 'conceptual analysis' approach to the philosophy of education had acquired all the characteristics of what, a few years earlier, Thomas Kuhn had called a 'paradigm': a 'received orthodoxy' that defines how a particular intellectual discipline is to be practised and understood.[8] What this particular paradigm most conspicuously demanded of those who wished to become 'philosophers of education' was that they repress any personal inclination to, in Eagleton's words, 'insist on posing to [our routine social practices] the most embarrassingly general and fundamental questions'. As, throughout the 1970s, this view of 'what the philosophy of education is' began to be imposed with greater totalitarian severity, so it quickly began to resemble something like a religious ideology to which anybody who aspired to become a philosopher of education was forced to subscribe.

Philosophies always bear the marks of the passage of time and, fortunately, the philosophy of education has been no exception. The ritual assertions about 'what philosophy is' that were so common in the 1970s now sound pretentious and absurd. And the various exclusionary tactics that were then used to marginalize those who refused to embrace the dominant analytic paradigm now serve only to marginalize its remaining adherents from everybody else. What, with hindsight, is also noticeable, is how the numerous philosophical inquiries that have been undertaken in the name of 'conceptual analysis' are now chiefly remarkable for what they have failed to achieve rather than for what they have. What they most obviously have failed to achieve is any significant success in settling the very questions about the meaning of educational concepts which the method of conceptual analysis claimed to be able to answer. Questions like 'what is education?', 'what is educational theory?' and 'how does educational theory relate to educational practice?' have all been discussed by philosophers of education of some distinction. But although the techniques of conceptual analysis allowed these philosophers to display a remarkably high level of technical skill, whenever and wherever they proceeded to provide substantial answers to the questions they posed, the results were always inconclusive and the points of disagreement have remained obstinately where they were. The net result has been that philosophy of education has now produced a number of equally impressive but mutually incompatible answers to precisely those 'conceptual' problems which it was designed to resolve.

This lack of any significant progress in pursuing its own research agenda has been matched by the failure of philosophy of education adequately to understand its relationship to its own past. For one of the characteristics of the philosophy of education has been to treat the past as a mere prelude to the present: as a source of philosophical and educational ideas that can be selectively plundered in order to deal with what *we* now take 'the problems of the philosophy of education' to be. As a result, illustrious predecessors – ranging from Plato to Dewey – are treated as participants in some contemporary philosophical discussion so that the philosophical perspective that *we* employ is superimposed on those that *they* employed in order to abstract what *we* now take to be their genuinely 'philosophical' insights from the more complex theoretical structures within which they were originally embedded. Given this way of interpreting its own history, it is unsurprising that educational philosophers of the past are treated in a manner which suggests that they were either philosophically immature or philosophically naive.[9] Nor is it surprising to find contemporary philosophers of education making patronizing excuses for the philosophical naivety of their predecessors by pointing to the culturally barren and intellectually retarded times in which it was their misfortune to live.

It was, of course, Hegel who most forcefully articulated the unfortunate implications of treating the history of philosophy in this way. If, on the one hand, we insist on always reading the philosophical past in terms of the philosophical present then we condemn ourselves to being selectively interpreted and misinterpreted by future generations of philosophers in much the same way that philosophers of the past are selectively interpreted and misinterpreted by the present generation. If, on the other hand, we choose to consign the history of philosophy to a separate discipline called 'the history of ideas' then we simply condemn our own philosophical arguments to becoming objects of antiquarian interest that will have no significant bearing on the contemporary discussions and debates of the future. In either case, the implication is the same: philosophers who refuse to situate themselves historically cannot avoid assigning themselves to future impotence and irrelevance.

For the philosophy of education, the loss incurred by its lack of historical self-consciousness has been two-fold. What, first has been lost is any sense of the philosophy of education as an activity which has continued from the time of Plato and hence as an activity in which even the most radical changes have occurred within a framework of continuity. Because most contemporary philosophers of education tend to think of themselves as engaging in an activity that only started in the 1960s, it is difficult for them to recognize anything that can be properly called the history of their discipline. It is thus hardly surprising that philosophies of education that pre-date the 1960s – such as those of Plato and Rousseau – are frequently dismissed as prehistory: part of that long period of premodern immaturity at the end of which modern philosophy of education finally emerged. Nor is it surprising that so many contemporary philosophers of education still think of themselves as the first true practitioners of their discipline rather than the latest participants in the much longer and larger process of philosophical transformation and educational change.

Thus what secondly has been lost is any adequate appreciation of contemporary philosophy of education as itself a socially embedded historical artefact that emerged out of a particular cultural climate and in response to fundamental intellectual problems and educational concerns. One inevitable consequence of this lack of historical self-consciousness is that the philosophy of education is unable to give a unified and continuous narrative account of itself. All it now seems able to offer is a series of isolated anecdotes about past educational philosophies designed primarily to show how they conflated genuinely 'philosophical' questions about education with 'empirical', 'ideological', 'practical' and other 'non philosophical' questions and concerns. But, of course, our understanding of what constitutes a 'genuinely philosophical question about education' has changed and understanding how, when and why it has changed is only possible from a philosophical perspective that has retained an interest in its own history. Within the contemporary philosophy of education any request to explain why it is that questions about education that were once labelled 'philosophical' are now labelled 'empirical', 'ideological' or 'practical' are usually treated as a pointless distraction that is of no 'philosophical' relevance or concern. Thus it is that so many contemporary philosophers of education now find themselves locked into a position whereby they can only consider their discipline historically by first relinquishing their own philosophical self-understanding.

For me, then, the process of becoming a philosopher of education has never been simply a matter of learning certain technical skills, adhering to an established paradigm, or conforming to a set of methodological rules. Like becoming a Catholic, it has been more a matter of learning to confront a historical tradition by participating in its dialogues and debates – dialogues and debates which have continued through past generations and which, therefore, have to be conducted not only with contemporary exponents of the discipline but also with those predecessors whose achievement it was to extend our understanding of this tradition to its present point. In my case, becoming a philosopher of education has required nothing other than that I became involved in the progressive working out of a historical tradition of intellectual inquiry and educational debate – a tradition which some contemporary philosophers of education may wish to discard and replace but to which they inevitably and unavoidably belong.

To suggest in this way that philosophers of education ought to become more historically self-conscious about their discipline is not to suggest that they should be engaged in a form of historical commentary that is unconcerned with rigorous philosophical analysis. Nor, incidentally, is it a suggestion that is in any way original. The claim that philosophy and the history of philosophy are one and the same was, of course, made with great force by Hegel and has subsequently been advanced by philosophers as different as Dewey, Collingwood, Gadamer and most recently Alisdaire MacIntyre and Charles Taylor.[10] However, despite its familiarity, it is a view that some philosophers of education may find incoherent, others may regard as unwelcome and only a few will want to endorse or share. But the crucial test for this view of the philosophy of education is not to be applied at the level of argument and counter-argument about 'what the philosophy of education is'. Rather it is to ask whether a historically informed philosophy of education can provide a superior understanding of the educational issues to which it is addressed than those ahistorical forms of philosophical inquiry that currently exist. The only way for me to answer this question is to point to my own efforts to write the kind of philosophy of education I have advocated and to invite comments on the extent to which I have either succeeded or failed.

PART I: THEORIZING
EDUCATION

1 THE GAP BETWEEN THEORY AND PRACTICE

Theory is vastly bigger than the province of intellectuals . . .
Everybody has a set of theories, compounded maybe of fact
and value, history and myth, observation and folklore,
superstition and convention . . . Those who refuse all theory,
who speak of themselves as plain, practical people, and
virtuous in virtue of having no theory, are in the grip of
theories which manacle them and keep them immobile,
because they have no way of thinking about them and
therefore of taking them off. They aren't theory-free; they are
stupid theorists.[1]

I

As a topic for discussion and debate, the relationship between educational
theory and educational practice has received more attention than most. In
consequence, there is an every-growing body of theoretical literature concerning such things as the logical relationship between theoretical statements and
practical principles and the contribution of academic disciplines to educational practice. Unfortunately, despite all this effort to explain how theory
should be related to practice, nothing seems to have changed and teachers
continue to cling to an image of theory as incomprehensible 'jargon' that has
nothing to do with their everyday problems and concerns. Ironically, it seems
that the impotence of any theoretical solution to the theory–practice issue is
guaranteed by the very problem it is designed to overcome.

Faced with this kind of situation, it is hardly surprising that some theorists
simply lose patience and account for their lack of practical impact in terms of

the ignorance, apathy or indifference of teachers. Others, however, realizing that their 'jargon' is often difficult to understand, and that the practical relevance of their theories is not always immediately obvious, acknowledge that there is a gap between theory and practice that can be bridged by introducing strategies which will bring relevant theories to the notice of teachers and convince them of their practical value. The purpose of this chapter is to suggest that the reason why educational theory has not had any significant impact on educational practice has little to do with teachers 'unhelpful' attitudes or with their inability to understand or implement theories. More positively, the intention is to argue that the gaps between theory and practice are firmly embedded in the conceptual foundations on which the whole practice of educational theorizing has been built and will only be eliminated by eliminating some of the dubious assumptions in terms of which educational theory and its relationship to practice have always been understood.

I would like to introduce and conclude this argument by making some general observations on the present scene which may help to clarify the essence of the position I wish to adopt. My prefatory observations concern the historical development of educational theory over the past two decades. During the 1960s, the then orthodox view of educational theory was subjected to a barrage of heavy-handed attacks by an army of philosophers and denounced as 'confused', 'vague', 'pseudo-theory'.[2] The revelation of these horrors led to educational theory being purged of its unacceptable features, and replaced by a somewhat arbitrary collection of academic disciplines. Before the end of the sixties these disciplines – the philosophy, psychology and sociology 'of education' – had managed to carve up their newly conquered domain among themselves.[3] Education departments were reorganized; courses were restructured; professional identities were changed; new journals and academic societies were established, all displaying total allegiance to the view that educational theory was nothing other than the application to education of these 'foundation' disciplines. During the early and mid-1970s, however, the puritanical zeal with which the disciplines approach had originally been pursued began to be tempered by a growing realization that many educational problems were not accessible from the narrow confines of any single theoretical discipline. Indeed, even the most ardent advocates of the approach began to concede that the hard won 'respectability' of educational theory might have been gained at the expense of 'relevance'.[4] As a result of these anxieties from within, the 'interdisciplinary', 'integrated' and 'problem-based' nature of educational theory was ritually asserted and the search was on for ways of bridging the gaps between educational theory and the practices that provide all this theory with its *raison d'être*.

This sequence of events – denunciation of the old order and strict allegiance to the new, followed by uneasy feelings that all is not well and furious efforts to put things right – is a familiar pattern in the history of ideas. I mention it in this context only to draw attention to the ways in which most solutions to the theory–practice problem have typically consisted of the kind of rearguard action taken to preserve and defend a *status quo* when confronted with its own failings and deficiencies. It is this kind of blanket refusal to envisage any alternative to the conception of educational theory that the current outlook embodies that most clearly distinguishes most of the arguments about the theory–practice problem from the argument I wish to pursue in this chapter. For running through my argument is the conviction that it is only by dismantling the faulty foundations on which the entire edifice of educational theory has been erected that basic questions about the theoretical study of education can begin to re-emerge and alternative answers can be reassessed.

II

At one time it was considered to be both theoretically possible and practically desirable to regard 'educational theory' as a set of practical principles derived from general philosophical beliefs.[5] In practice, the usual way of generating this sort of theory was to outline the metaphysical, epistemological and ethical theses of influential philosophers and then to extract some 'educational implications' which could serve as guiding principles for educational practitioners. Originally, the most popular of the 'Great Educators' were Plato and Rousseau, but these were soon joined by others such as Herbart, Froebel and Pestalozzi, and by a large ancillary literature that described and evaluated their central doctrines.

The most common complaints levelled at this kind of educational theory pointed to the wide gap that existed between the abstract and highly general principles that it produced and the concrete situations that teachers actually faced in classrooms. However, the main reason why the approach was eventually discarded was not because it was perceived by practitioners as being unrelated to the practices it was supposed to guide, but because of criticisms directed at its methodological assumptions by modern analytic philosophy. For example, the criticisms made in the late 1950s by D. J. O'Connor and other scientifically minded philosophers were intended not to close the gap that had emerged between theory and practice but to demonstrate that the claim of this kind of educational theory to have any significant 'practical implications' was logically unsound.[6]

In denying that educational theory had any overriding practical purpose, O'Connor's intention was to confine future educational theorizing to the production of empirically established findings. However, the philosophical account that emerged to govern contemporary approaches to educational theory refused to accept the kind of restrictions that O'Connor had prescribed and adopted the view that educational theory was a species of 'practical theory' with a different purpose and structure from that of scientific theory. For example, Paul Hirst, the major exponent of this view, argued that educational theory should not be limited to the scientific objectives of prediction and explanation but rather should be 'concerned to determine and guide' educational practices. Consequently, the source of educational theory should not be limited to scientific knowledge but should instead 'draw on' various 'forms of knowledge', particularly philosophy, history and morality as well as the social sciences.[7]

What is worth noticing is that, despite their differences, the various conceptions of educational theory that have emerged over the past thirty years all endorse certain basic assumptions about the nature of educational theory and its relationship to educational practice. For example, although opinions about what constitutes the proper source of educational theory have changed from philosophy to science and then to a collection of 'forms of knowledge', the basic assumption that educational theory should be 'derived from' or 'based on' *some* already existing academic theory has never been seriously disputed. Similarly, while views about the extent to which educational theory can legitimately guide practice have varied, it has always been supposed that its purpose is to formulate general principles that can then be applied by teachers in order to solve their problems and improve their practices. Yet the belief that educational theory must conform to conventional criteria of academic adequacy overlooks the point that a theoretical enterprise does not acquire legitimacy simply by adopting the methods, findings or criteria of another theoretical enterprise, but by demonstrating a capacity to explore a particular range of problems in a systematic and rigorous manner. The important question to be asked, therefore, is not one about the kind of academic theory on which educational theory should depend, but the logically prior question of whether a theoretical enterprise concerned with a practical activity like education should be so intrinsically dependent on academic disciplines at all.

III

The concept of 'theory' has, of course, numerous connotations, and definitions range from the strict scientific interpretations ('a set of logically connected and verified hypotheses') to much looser and wider meanings ('a way of looking at objects and information'). As far as theoretical activities themselves are concerned, however, 'theory' can have at least two distinct meanings. On the one hand, it can refer to the actual products of theoretical inquiries and, when used in this way, it is usually presented in the form of general principles, laws, explanations and the like. On the other hand, 'theory' can refer to the framework of thought that structures and guides any distinctive theoretical activity. Used in this sense, it denotes the underlying conceptual framework in terms of which a particular theoretical enterprise is carried out and which provides it with its general rationale. Phrases like 'psychological theory' or 'sociological theory' are, therefore, somewhat ambiguous. They can identify both the theoretical knowledge produced by those who engage in psychological or sociological inquiry (such as a theory of learning or a theory of organizations) and the particular ways of thinking that guide the practices of those engaged in psychological or sociological pursuits (such as the behaviourist theory or the interactionist theory). In effect, then, the 'theories' that arise out of activities like psychology and sociology are no more than the formally stated outcomes of practices that are themselves guided by 'theories' which express how those who engage in these practices ought to proceed.

For psychologists, sociologists and others engaged in theoretical pursuits, practical problems can arise when conventional ways of conducting theoretical inquiries and investigations are, in particular instances, found to be inadequate to their purpose. In other words, gaps between 'theory' and 'practice' can occur when the procedures normally employed in theoretical undertakings are unsuitable to a given situation. Usually, these are regarded as 'methodological' problems about such things as the appropriateness of particular methods of collecting data or the usefulness of certain research techniques and they are invariably resolved by making modifications to normal practice in ways that are likely to ensure that the desired outcome is successfully achieved.

In the main, the gaps between the theory and the practice of a theoretical activity are such that they can be closed by taking action that is consistent with the basic procedural principles incorporated in the theoretical framework guiding the activity in question. However, it is possible that the gaps may be resistant to these kinds of modifications and require changes of a more basic kind. More specifically, the practices normally employed in a theoretical activity may eventually be perceived to be so incompatible with its overall guiding principles and values that the entire theoretical framework – or 'paradigm' – underlying conventional methods is called into question and discarded.[8] This kind of rejection of an established mode of theoretical practice was evident in developments in sociological theory during the early 1970s. At that time, there was a growing dissatisfaction with the capacity of the established theory of sociological analysis to realize the general sociological aim of understanding social reality. Because it relied on methodological principles that paid insufficient attention to the way in which social reality is constructed through the activities of social actors, the kind of functionist paradigm that had largely dominated sociological inquiries became questionable and gave way to a theoretical approach that guided the practices of sociologists in a completely 'new direction'.[9] Needless to say, when this kind of change occurs, it entails changes in methods and practices which are so fundamental that the nature and scope of the whole enterprise are perceived in an entirely different way.

IV

Education is not, of course, a theoretical activity, but a practical activity concerned with the general task of developing pupils' minds through the processes of teaching and learning. However, although it is unlike psychology or sociology in that it is not concerned with the production of theories and explanations, education is similar to theoretical practices in being a consciously performed intentional activity that can only be understood by reference to the framework of thought in terms of which its practitioners make sense of what they are doing and what it is that they are trying to achieve. In this sense, anybody engaged in educational pursuits must, no less than anybody engaged in theoretical pursuits, already possess some 'theory' in virtue of which his or her practices are conducted and achievements assessed. Further, the theories that guide theoretical practices and those guiding educational practices share certain common features. Both, for example, are largely the product of existing and ongoing traditions and, as such, constitute the ways of conceptualizing experience that are regarded as appropriate for the social contexts within which the respective practices are undertaken. Hence, the fact that the guiding theory of a theoretical practice may be largely acquired through a deliberate and systematic introduction to 'methodology' does not alter the fact that it is, no less than a theory of educational practice, an inherited and accepted way of thinking. Second, each mode of thought employs an interrelated set of concepts, beliefs, assumptions and values that allow situations and events to be interpreted in ways that are appropriate to their separate concerns. For example, while both psychological and educational practices may be structured around concepts like 'learning', 'intelligence', 'interest' and the like, their meanings will differ with the different conceptual schemes within which their interpretation takes place.

As with theoretical activities, problems occur for educational practitioners when their methods and procedures are no longer effective. These gaps between theory and practice may occur when, for example, the value of traditional methods of assessment is no longer evident or when some standard teaching method is found to be unsuccessful in a new situation, and they are usually resolved by practitioners modifying their practices in the light of the framework of understanding that they have already acquired. However, as with theoretical pursuits, the gaps may be such that they raise questions not only about the effectiveness of specific practices but also about the capacity of the conceptual framework within which these practices are understood to provide a satisfactory characterization of educational activities at all. For example, dissatisfaction with 'traditional' educational practices led some educators to reappraise the basic patterns of thought in terms of which this kind of education is made intelligible and regarded as desirable. It also led Dewey and others to introduce notions like 'interaction', 'continuity', 'growth' and 'experience', and so provide the kind of conceptual background against which an entirely different view of what constitutes an educational practice could be defined and defended.

When 'theory' and 'practice' are looked at in this way, it becomes increasingly obvious that the gaps between them that usually cause concern are not those occurring between a practice and the theory guiding that practice, but rather those that arise because it is assumed that 'educational theory' refers to theories other than those that already guide educational pursuits. For example, the 'communication gap' between theorists and practitioners only arises because the language of educational theory is not the language of educational practice. Similarly, the gaps between educational theory and its practical application can only exist because practitioners do not interpret or evaluate the theories that they are offered according to the criteria utilized by those engaged in theoretical pursuits.

The problem with this whole conception of educational theory is that it fails to recognize the extensive theoretical powers that educational practitioners already possess and thereby distorts, in several important respects, the relationship between theory and practice and the way in which gaps between them can occur. For example, to regard theory–practice gaps as problems of 'communication' or 'implementation' that are peculiar to practical activities like education distorts the fact that a gap between theory and practice is the kind of difficulty that can also occur in the course of any theoretical undertaking. Second, the assumption that these difficulties can somehow be identified and tackled 'in theory' and then 'applied' in practice tends to conceal how they are generated out of the experience of practitioners and only emerge when the way in which these experiences are usually organized is found to be ineffective. Third, the view that the problems that these gaps create can be overcome by converting theoretical knowledge into rules of action, or 'practical principles', overlooks the simple point that gaps between theory and practice, whether they occur for theoreticians or for educators, are closed by the practitioners themselves formulating decisions in the light of the framework of understanding that they already possess. It also overlooks the fact that, since it is only educational practitioners who actually engage in educational pursuits, it is the theory guiding their practice rather than the theory guiding any theoretical practice that constitutes the source of their educational principles, determines if and when any gaps between practice and these principles exist and informs any decisions and actions that are taken to achieve their resolution.

The important points that need to be recognized, then, can be summarized like this. The gaps between theory and practice which everyone deplores are actually endemic to the view that educational theory can be produced from within theoretical and practical contexts different from the theoretical and practical context within which it is supposed to apply. Because this sort of view is so widespread, it is hardly surprising that the gaps thereby created are interpreted as impediments that can only be removed by finding ways of inducing teachers to accept and apply the theory that they are being offered. If, however, it is recognized that there is nothing to which the phrase 'educational theory' can coherently refer other than the theory that actually guides educational practices, then it becomes apparent that a theoretical activity explicitly concerned to influence educational practice can only do so by influencing the theoretical framework in terms of which these practices are made intelligible.

On this view, then, educational theory is not an 'applied theory' that 'draws on' theories from philosophy, social science or any other 'form of knowledge', but rather refers to the whole enterprise of critically appraising the adequacy of the concepts, beliefs, assumptions and values incorporated in prevailing theories of educational practice. This does not mean that the relationship of theory to practice is such that theory 'implies' practice, or is 'derived' from practice or even 'reflects' practice. Rather, by subjecting the beliefs and justifications of existing and ongoing practical traditions to rational criticism, theory transforms practice by transforming the ways in which practice is experienced and understood. The transition is not, therefore, from theory to practice as such, but from irrationality to rationality, from ignorance and habit to knowledge and reflection. Further, if educational theory is interpreted in this way, closing the gap between theory and practice is not a matter of improving the practical effectiveness of the products of theoretical activities, but one of improving the practical effectiveness of the theories that teachers employ in conceptualizing their own activities. Reducing the gaps between theory and practice is thus the central aim of educational theory rather than something that needs to be done after the theory has been produced but before it can be effectively applied.

What this implies is that any educational theory that takes the purpose of its own activity seriously should be directed towards providing educational practitioners with the intellectual resources that will enable them to take their activities more seriously. A basic feature of educational theory so understood is that it seeks to emancipate practitioners from their dependence on practices that are the product of precedent, habit and tradition by developing modes of analysis and inquiry that are aimed at exposing and examining the beliefs, values and assumptions implicit in the theoretical framework through which practitioners organize their experiences. It is only by so challenging the adequacy of conventional theories of educational practice that the observations, interpretations and judgements of practitioners will become more rational and coherent and their practices will be conducted in more disciplined, intelligent and effective ways.

V

What, so far, I have tried to show is how the conventional gaps between theory and practice are due to the failure of prevailing views of educational theory to offer adequate criteria for distinguishing theory that is genuinely educational from theory of a purely academic or scientific character. Consequently, I have argued that attempts to remedy the situation by introducing 'problem-based' or 'integrated' approaches that are designed to bridge these gaps are entirely misguided. In these final paragraphs I would like to suggest some of the basic features that a more adequate conception of educational theory would need to incorporate, and to indicate some of the measures that its implementation would seem to require.

In the first place, if educational theory is rooted in the knowledge that it is the need to resolve educational problems that provides its purpose and rationale, then it will be organized by an awareness of how any approach that transforms these problems into a series of theoretical questions merely deprives them of their essentially practical character and thereby misconceives the purpose of the whole enterprise. Implicit in this view, therefore, is the realization that there are no 'educational disciplines' as such and that any approach that uses educational problems as a convenient entrance to philosophy, psychology and sociology simply puts the finishing touches to a general move in the wrong direction. The practical problems of education are no more solved by importing the solutions to theoretical problems offered by psychology and sociology than the practical or 'methodological' problems of psychology and sociology are solved by importing conclusions arrived at in the philosophy of mind or the philosophy of science.

Second, what is distinctive about the kind of educational theory being envisaged is that it stems from a recognition of the fact that the problems it seeks to confront only arise for and can only be resolved by educational practitioners. As a result, it acknowledges that success in educational theory is entirely dependent on the extent to which teachers can be encouraged to develop a more refined and effective understanding of their own problems and practices. It is, therefore, entirely inappropriate for educational theorists to treat teachers as objects for theoretical inspection or as clients who accept and apply theoretical solutions. Rather, since the practical experience of teachers is the source of the problems under consideration, it must be recognized that the active participation of practitioners in the theoretical enterprise is an indispensable necessity.

Third, in so far as educational theory seeks to help practitioners to confront their problems more effectively, the concrete practical experiences out of which these problems are generated provides both the subject matter for theoretical inquiry and the testing ground on which the results of this inquiry must be assessed. Hence, it must be recognized that theory only acquires an 'educational' status when it suggests improved ways of understanding these experiences and only acquires educational validity when these suggestions are tested and confirmed by practical experience. What this means is that the idea that theory can be devised and tested independently of practice and then used to correct, improve or assess any educational practice is rejected in favour of the diametrically opposite view that theory only acquires an educational character in so far as it can itself be corrected, improved and assessed in the light of its practical consequences. In this sense, it is practice that determines the value of any educational theory, rather than theory that determines the value of any educational practice.

Once it is conceded that to undertake a theoretical activity like psychology or sociology, or a practical activity like education, involves engaging in some recognizable set of practices, and once it is acknowledged that these practices are not, any more than are human observations, free from theoretical preconceptions, then it becomes apparent that 'educational theory' is not something that is created in isolation from practice and then has to be 'applied', 'implemented' or 'adopted' through a sustained effort on the part of the two reluctant parties. 'Education' is not some kind of inert phenomenon that can be observed, isolated, explained and theorized about. There are no 'educational phenomena' apart from the practices of those engaged in educational activities, no 'educational problems' apart from those arising from these practices and no 'educational theories' apart from those that structure and guide these practices. The only task which 'educational theory' can legitimately pursue, then, is to develop theories of educational practice that are intrinsically related to practitioners' own accounts of what they are doing, that will improve the quality of their involvement in these practices and thereby allow them to practise better.

Finally, I would like to return to my promised postscript about some of the more general features of the way in which the theory–practice issue is normally discussed. Underlying and infecting most of the arguments and counter-arguments surrounding this whole issue, there seems to be an instinctive fear that to dispense with the academic disciplines would strip educational theory of all its claims to validity, cogency and truth. What I have tried to show is that capitulating to this fear not only gives 'theory' sole custody of these intellectual virtues but simultaneously consigns 'practice' to a certain indignity and worthlessness. Itself deprived of academic status and intellectual rigour, practice is sentenced to a permanent dependence on some external 'theory' for the systematic cogent thinking that, in itself, it so sadly lacks. It is only when this separation of 'pure' theory from 'impure' practice has been successfully accomplished that the 'problem' arises of finding some way of reuniting them. Of course, any proposals to do this which regard practice as a source of theory in its own right must be strenuously resisted. If they are not resisted – if practice is itself credited with theoretical attributes – then its slavish reliance on academic disciplines would become redundant and all the proverbial 'gaps' would disappear.

This desire to drive a wedge between theory and practice has a long and illustrious history. It is, in part, a legacy of Plato's attempt to erect a high-order domain of perfect 'Forms' which would correct the imperfections of ordinary beliefs and actions. It is also implicit in Kant's idea of a transcendental, noumenal 'self' stipulating absolute standards to which the earth-bound, phenomenal self should conform. Now, as always, Plato and Kant are attacked for their dualism. Now, as always, the hierarchical and divisive mode of thinking which they bequeathed is criticized and repudiated. However, despite this official demise, the untenable divisions between knowing and doing, thought and action, continue to pervade and distort the study of education. The idea of educational theory as something that guides educational practice without itself being guided by practice, as something that solves practical problems without itself being penetrated by practical problems, lives on. It is displayed in the way in which philosophy, psychology and sociology offer themselves as a unique source of understanding and as specialist agencies for solving educational problems. It is further reinforced by the way in which the deliberate isolation of 'value-free' theory from 'value-laden' practice is taken as a sure sign that those running the 'theory' side of things have the right intellectual and academic credentials.

There are many objectionable things about this kind of segregation of theory from practice but what is worth stressing is this. Until educational theory ceases to confine itself to forms of theorizing whose relationship to what is being theorized about is never fully considered, then it will always leave untouched the dominant discourse of educational practice and so leave untouched its claim to articulate the way that education is and should be. It is the discourse of educational practice, not the discourse of some theoretical practice, that structures the perceptions of educational practitioners and hence structures educational reality itself. When teachers refer to 'classroom control' and when they talk about 'getting children to work or behave better', they subscribe to particular interpretations of educational situations which may or may not be adequate but which could always have been different. The very concepts of educational practice are part of that practice and the very emergence of a form of words as an acceptable description of an educational situation (is it a problem of 'control' or 'bad teaching' or 'a lack of interest'?) further shapes that situation and so shapes the kind of decisions and actions taken to improve or change it. It is for this reason that any educational theory that takes itself seriously cannot confine itself to the official discourse of theoretical disciplines, nor rest content with defining yet another academic category into which yet another body of theoretical information can be harmlessly deposited. Rather, it must strive to examine the adequacy of the concepts and theories that are embodied in the language of educational practice by articulating the relationship of educational discourse to the realities that this discourse purports to capture and describe. This does not involve transforming educational theory into an unstructured mixture of theorizing and practice. Nor does it imply that educational theory must be restricted to 'the classroom'. Still less does it mean that philosophy, psychology and sociology have no part to play and should be resisted.[10] What has to be resisted is the temptation to interpret educational theory in terms of conventional notions of theoretical purity and in conformity with the existing classification of academic disciplines. Educational theory will only begin to realize its original promise when it abandons its self-imposed isolation, its self-complacent practical ignorance and its self-indulgent search for academic status. In education, theory is an indispensable dimension of practice.

2 THEORIES OF
THEORY AND
PRACTICE

Theory is just a practice forced into a new form of self-reflectiveness . . . Theory is just human activity bending back upon itself, constrained into a new kind of self-reflexivity. And, in absorbing this self-reflexivity, the activity itself will be transformed.[1]

I

Questions about educational theory tend to cluster into two quite different areas of concern. On the one hand, there are philosophical issues concerning the logical structure of educational theory – issues concerning, for example, the scientific status of educational theory and its relationship to the 'foundation' disciplines. On the other hand, there are non-philosophical problems about how educational theory should be used in relation to educational practice – problems, for example, about whether educational theory should be presented as 'topic based' or 'problem based' or about how it can best be deployed in the preparation and professional development of teachers. The fact that these two areas of concern are normally treated separately is unsurprising for at least two reasons. First, it more or less accurately reflects the existing division of labour between those engaged in the theoretical study of education (educational studies) and those whose primary concern is to relate these theoretical studies to the problems of educational practice (professional studies). Second, the separation of philosophical questions concerning the 'logic' of educational theory from organizational questions concerning its presentation and use, is itself just a particular instance of the modern disposition to draw a sharp distinction between 'theoretical' issues concerning the nature of knowledge and 'non-theoretical' issues concerning the practical purposes to which this knowledge should be put.[2]

What I am going to suggest is that so long as this distinction remains rooted in our understanding of educational theory, so long will our understanding be distorted and impaired. For what this distinction effectively conceals is how 'philosophical' questions about the nature of educational theory and 'non-philosophical' questions about how this theory relates to practice are not two separate questions at all. The fundamental reason why this is so is that ideas about the nature of educational theory are always ideas about the nature of educational practice and always incorporate a latent conception of how, in practice, theory should be used. Thus the systematic, well articulated and explicit accounts of educational theory which philosophers are prone to discuss and dissect are, at one and the same time, less systematic, unarticulated and often implicit accounts of educational practice as well. There are not, therefore, theories of theory and theories of practice and yet other theories about the relationship between the two. All educational theories are theories of theory and practice.

If this claim is correct then the theory and practice of education will have to be construed in ways somewhat different from those which philosophers and theorists usually recognize or admit. For it follows from this claim that philosophers should no longer discuss questions about the 'logic' of educational theory in isolation from questions about the 'logic' of educational practice. It also follows that educational theorists should no longer view educational practice in one way for the purpose of its theoretical study and in a different way when they consider how, in practice, the fruits of their studies may be used. It is, therefore, worth considering how this claim can be made good.

II

Consider, first, what it is to engage in an educational practice. Clearly, an educational practice is not some kind of robot-like behaviour that can be performed in a completely unthinking or mechanical way. It is a consciously performed intentional activity which can only be made intelligible by reference to the often tacit and, at best, partially articulated schemes of thought in terms of which practitioners make sense of their experiences. Hence, practitioners are only able to engage in educational practices by virtue of their ability to characterize their own practice and construe the practices of others in ways that presuppose, usually implicitly, a set of beliefs about what they are doing, the situation in which they are operating and what it is they are trying to achieve. These beliefs may be more or less coherent and systematic, and the more coherent and systematic they are, the more closely they resemble a 'theory'. This is not to say that there is some observable 'practice' and some non-observable 'theory' in the minds of practitioners. Rather, it is simply to make the point that to engage in an educational practice always presupposes a theoretical scheme that is at one and the same time constitutive of this practice and the means for understanding the educational practices of others.

It is also to make the point that an educational practice is a social practice and, hence, that the theoretical scheme of an individual practitioner is not something that can be acquired in isolation. Rather, it is a way of thinking that is learned from, and shared with, other practitioners and preserved by those traditions of educational thought and practice within which it has developed and evolved. In other words, the theoretical schemes of educational practitioners have a history: they are the inherited ways of thinking into which practitioners must be initiated if what they think, say and do is to be structured in an intelligent and coherent way.[3]

Consider, secondly, what it is to engage in a theoretical practice like psychology, sociology or philosophy. To undertake any one of these pursuits is to engage in a distinctive social activity by means of specific procedures and skills and in accordance with the way of thinking and acting appropriate to the institutional setting in which this activity is pursued. Each of these ways of thinking and acting incorporates an interrelated set of beliefs and assumptions providing rules and maxims which operate both as instructions about how events and situations are to be interpreted and as prescriptions about how to proceed if one's practice is to be interpreted by others as the practice of a theoretical activity of a particular sort. Thus, phrases like 'psychological theory' and 'sociological theory' can be used both to denote the theoretical end-products of those engaged in psychological or sociological inquiries (such as a psychological theory of learning) and the particular theoretical frameworks guiding the inquiries of those engaged in psychological or sociological pursuits (such as behaviourism). In short, the 'theories' arising out of psychology and sociology are no more than the formally stated outcome of practices that are themselves guided by theories which express how those engaged in these practices ought to proceed.

Consider, finally, those all too familiar occasions when educational practitioners read theoretical interpretations of what they are doing which are very different from their own. That such discrepancies exist is, of course, entirely predictable. For while the degree of intelligibility of a practitioner's self-understanding of his or her practice is invariably the degree to which it coincides with the theoretical preconceptions of other educational practitioners, the educational theorist's interpretation is apt to coincide with the theoretical presumptions informing whatever perspectives are currently fashionable or otherwise deemed appropriate. It should, therefore, come as no surprise to find that there are certain difficulties in relating educational theory to educational practice. What is surprising is the extent to which this difficulty is still seen as a 'gap' between theory and practice rather than a gap between rival theories about how educational practice is to be understood.[4] It is for similar reasons that the image of educational theory as a form of interdisciplinary cooperation has failed to materialize. Indeed, given that the ways in which educational psychology understands educational practice are very different from the understandings of educational sociology, and that both are different from the understandings adopted in educational philosophy, it is difficult to know how any attempt to establish this kind of interdisciplinary research programme could ever get off the ground.

Looked at in this way it is not too difficult to see why rival interpretations of educational theory are rooted in rival interpretations of educational practice. No practice is what it is independently of what its practitioners think or believe about it and this is just as true for the practice of theoretical pursuits as it is for practical pursuits like education. Moreover, just as educational practice cannot be undertaken without practitioners thinking about (and hence theorizing about) what they are doing, so it cannot be observed by educational theorists in a theory-neutral way. This does not just mean that different kinds of educational theory tend to 'imply' different forms of educational practice. Nor does it mean that educational theory can be 'derived from' or 'based on' educational practice. Rather it means that there is no way for educational theory to characterize educational practice which is both theoretically neutral and capable of rendering the practice thus characterized intelligible.

Once it is conceded that to undertake a theoretical activity like psychology or a practical activity like education always involves engaging in some recognizable set of human practices, and once it is acknowledged that these practices are not, any more than human observations, free from theoretical preconceptions, then it becomes clear why any attempt to create a body of educational theory in isolation from practice and then relate it to some nontheoretical world of practice, is, at best, misguided. It also becomes clear why rival views of educational theory incorporate rival views of how theory relates to practice. One of the obvious implications of the argument so far advanced is that a conception of educational theory, in so far as it supports a conception of educational practice, also delimits the kind of theory–practice relationship it is deemed appropriate to adopt. The reason why this is so is that the conceptual schemes employed in the theoretical study of education always construe practice in a way which ensures that the products of such study are of practical relevance and use. Thus, it is unsurprising to find that where the theorist interprets practice in a similar way to the practitioner, theory will relate to practice in a relevant way. Where, however, the theorist and practitioner construe practice in radically different ways, theory is, from the perspective of the practitioner, perceived as unrelated to practice and irrelevant to his or her practical problems and concerns.

So far the main burden of my argument has been to show that when critical attention is focused on the connection between the practice of educational theorizing and the educational practices to which this theorizing is addressed, it becomes clear that educational theory not only identifies educational practice, but also shapes and defines practice as well. It follows from this that questions about the nature of educational theory and questions about the nature of educational practice are logically linked. It also follows that questions about how educational theory changes practice are not independent of questions about how educational theory is to be understood.

To this point my argument has rested on a philosophical analysis aimed at illuminating the *a priori* assumptions inherent in theoretical and practical activities and at drawing out some of the implications of this analysis for our understanding of how educational theory and practice are interrelated. Although educational theorizing necessarily presupposes the assumptions I have sought to elucidate, this does not mean that educational theorists must have formulated them in any self-conscious way. For educational theorists to deny that they were committed to either a particular view of practice or a particular view of how their theories relate to practice would not, therefore, invalidate my argument. All that it would show is the extent to which educational theorists had considered the presuppositions of their activity in a reflective or philosophical way.

At the same time, however, the fact that my argument is philosophical and abstract does not mean that it is entirely impervious to empirical assessment. It would be a serious refutation to my argument if the kind of approaches to educational theory that are currently employed could not be shown to bear the relationship to educational practice that I have argued they must have. It is, therefore, incumbent upon me to illustrate my thesis by reference to the ways in which educational theorizing is commonly practised and understood. This I intend to do by describing the different ways in which four teachers 'theorized' their own practice in a manner which makes explicit the view of 'practice' they incorporate and the view of the theory–practice relationship they sustain.

III

Susan Hughes, John Smith, David Evans and Mary Jones all worked in comprehensive schools that were formed in the 1960s. As participants in a university-based course on educational studies, they all decided to undertake a 'school-based' study as a basis for deciding what changes and improvements they could make to their mixed ability teaching in their schools.

The first of these teachers, Susan Hughes, taught modern languages and, although she felt competent and confident when teaching older pupils in 'streamed classes', she also felt that she lacked the skill and expertise to teach the younger mixed ability classes. She thought that the best way to acquire this skill and expertise was by learning from other more experienced modern language teachers who had developed various strategies, methods and techniques for handling the kind of problems she was experiencing. To this end, she began to read various documents and reports – such as the reports of school inspectors on the teaching of modern languages and the documents on 'good practice' in modern language teaching produced by her own professional 'subject' association. From this body of literature she began to distil a list of practical recommendations about how to organize and teach modern languages to mixed ability groups which seemed to address her own particular concerns. She then incorporated these suggestions into her own mixed ability teaching to see if they helped her to improve her own classroom performance. Finally she wrote a descriptive report outlining what she had done and highlighting the practical value of the various ideas and suggestions that she had tried out.

John Smith was a mathematics teacher and, like the rest of the mathematics department, he had some doubts about mixed ability teaching for his own subject. The school policy was to run a 'mixed economy' so that for some subjects it was common in years one to three while others streamed and set after year two. But in mathematics (and French) mixed ability only operated in year one. John and his mathematics colleagues were under pressure to 'go mixed ability' in year two. John suspected that the arguments supporting this pressure were 'ideological' rather than 'educational' and that the proposed changes in second-year mathematics were based on personal bias rather than impersonal facts. He believed that any innovation needed to be based on sound scientific knowledge about how well children in mixed ability groups learn mathematics. He therefore measured the ability of all second year pupils by using a standard IQ test. Then, he compared the rate of progress in mathematics made by pupils in groups selected on the basis of ability with that of pupils in groups selected from across the ability range. Since his findings showed that able pupils make less progress when they are put in genuine mixed ability groups, and that weak pupils learn mathematics more effectively when they are grouped together, this provided him with an objective justification for grouping the pupils in mixed ability classes according to their ability. On the basis of this, John wrote a report recommending a mathematics policy for second-year mixed ability groups together with certain practical recommendations for implementing this policy.

David Evans was an English teacher and, although (unlike John Smith) he was an enthusiastic supporter of mixed ability teaching, it posed him some difficulties. His third-year mixed ability teaching did not seem to be working as it should, though he did not really understand why. Part of his worry was the way in which classroom discussions about some piece of literature always seemed to be dominated by the bright pupils. Despite his best intentions, the low-ability pupils did not really participate. He wanted to change things so that pupils of all ability would participate on equal terms.

To this end, David began to formulate some interesting questions. 'Who talks to whom in my classroom discussions?' 'Do I talk to some pupils more than others?' 'Who are they?' 'Do exchanges with pupils vary according to my presumptions about their ability?' In order to get to grips with these questions, David started collecting various kinds of data. First, he transcribed a series of tape recordings of classroom discussion with his third-year mixed ability group. Second, he devised an observation schedule to record the type of questions he asks ('open' or 'closed'; 'factual' or 'explanatory') and his responses to how questions are answered ('encouraging and affirmative' or 'discouraging and negative').

As he sifted through all these data, David tried to sort out what they meant and to crystallize his thoughts. Certain of the things revealed were real 'eye openers'. For example, he noticed that whenever he asked a factual question he seemed to direct it towards a 'low-ability' child, whereas 'explanatory' questions went to those pupils he thought to be 'bright'. The data also revealed several things about the quality of pupils' responses – about how pupils avoid answering questions and about how he sometimes uses questions for the purpose of transmitting factual information rather than creating a genuine discussion. David wrote up his findings in the form of a case study: a reflective account written in a naturalistic, informal style and containing various insights which helped to illuminate and explain what was going on in his classroom. He then used this case study as the basis for a series of discussions with other teachers about how better to promote the aims and values of mixed ability.

Mary Jones taught history. Like David Evans she was keen on mixed ability teaching. What worried her was that many of the problems of streaming and selection which mixed ability teaching was supposed to do something about still remained. The aspirations behind the abolition of streaming – greater individual fulfilment and greater equality of opportunity – seem somehow to have got left behind. Mixed ability teaching did not seem to have made education any less competitive or any less hierarchical or any more egalitarian. Generally, things had got no better; if anything, they had got worse.

Mary therefore decided that she wanted to examine some of the obvious contradictions to which mixed ability gave rise. 'Why is there a "gap" between the educational values and principles which mixed ability teaching is supposed to promote, and the way in which it actually operates in my school?' 'What constrains mixed ability teaching so that it remains incapable of reducing the kind of injustices and inequalities that it was designed to counteract?'

As with David Evans, Mary's first step was to collect different kinds of qualitative data about mixed ability teaching practices in her own school. But she also felt that it was important to locate the data in a broader political, cultural and historical context. In particular, she wanted to try to explore the tensions she experienced between her mixed ability teaching and the all-pervading influence of the framework of ideas and beliefs that constitute what is generally known as 'meritocracy'. What Mary intended to do was to examine her research data from a perspective which (unlike that of John Smith) did not treat meritocracy as a scientific verified theory about individual differences in ability. Instead, she wanted to regard meritocracy as an ideology: a historically contingent and culturally specific set of beliefs and practices which, in principle, allowed streaming to be made consistent with the principle of equality of opportunity but which, in practice, still allowed schools to continue to allocate opportunities in an unfair and unequal way.

To this end, Mary also wrote a case study. But as well as being reflective and insightful, it was critical and historical: critical not in the sense of simply carping about the status quo but in the sense of exposing to critical analysis those inherited beliefs and assumptions which are transmitted through history and tradition and which still govern contemporary educational policies and practices. Mary's case study thus took the form of a critical history of mass schooling – a history which was sensitive to the social and political context out of which mixed ability teaching had developed and evolved.

Although these four sketches may leave a lot to be desired they are nevertheless sufficient to make it possible to identify the different approaches to educational theory they each incorporate and the different view of the theory–practice relationship they each sustain.

The 'common sense' approach

This is the approach adopted by Susan Hughes. Both in theory and in practice this approach is quickly gaining acceptance by members of the teaching profession, teacher educators whose allegiance is to a particular teaching subject, politicians, policy-makers and many members of HM Inspectorate. As its name indicates, it refers to all those approaches that attempt to ground educational theory in the common-sense understandings of practitioners.[5]

What is definitive of this approach is the basic assumption that the notion of educational theory can be articulated from within the world of practice: for since, on this view, practice incorporates its own concepts and beliefs, educational theory can rest content with identifying, codifying and testing the 'practical principles' in which these concepts and beliefs are expressed. Such 'practical principles' are not, therefore, generalizations derived from, or tested by, educational theory. On the contrary, they are generalizations acquired through the observation and analysis of practice and tested pragmatically in practical situations. The idea that educational theory can be devised independently of practice and then used to assess practice is, therefore, replaced by the diametrically opposite view that theory must itself be tested and corrected in the light of its practical consequences. It is practice that determines the validity of theory rather than theory that determines the validity of practice.

Construed in this way, theory relates to practice by recovering the concepts, principles and skills implicit in 'good practice' and using these as a basis both for the recognition of practical competence and for the correction of deficiencies in practical performance. Thus, critical questions about the educational value of any practice are regarded as empirical questions that can be answered by reference to practical principles distilled from the activities of those who are already regarded as successful practitioners of educational pursuits. The question of what constitutes an *educational* practice is, on this view, a largely uncontentious issue. To engage in an educational practice is to think and act in conformity with the concepts, knowledge and skills of a given tradition.

The 'applied science' approach

This is the approach of John Smith. It is favoured by educational psychologists of a behaviourist persuasion, objectives-based curriculum theorists, educational researchers in the 'traditional' paradigm and all those who insist that any defensible notion of educational theory must conform to standards laid down by science.[6] Thus, it is axiomatic in this approach that educational phenomena are amenable to scientific methods of investigation and that the logical criteria of a scientific explanation provide the standards which educational theory must strive to achieve. So understood, educational theory is a form of 'applied science' using empirically tested generalizations as a basis for resolving educational problems and guiding educational practice.

Because some educational problems involve judgements about worthwhile ends, it is always necessary within this approach to separate questions of 'means' from questions of 'ends' and relate this to a parallel distinction between 'facts' and 'values'. Once this distinction is made, it becomes clear that since problems about educational ends involve judgements of value which cannot be settled scientifically, they cannot be a legitimate concern of educational theory. However, questions about the most effective means to achieve worthwhile ends are always factual questions, and, as such, can be settled objectively on the basis of sound scientific knowledge.

It is because it incorporates this instrumental 'means–end' view of education that this approach always interprets educational practice as an essentially technical activity designed to bring about the achievement of specifiable educational ends. 'Good practice' is not, therefore, determined by reference to the practical principles inherent in a given tradition, but by reference to those scientific principles by means of which desirable educational outcomes can be most effectively produced.

Thus, in the 'applied science' approach, theory does not relate to practice by drawing on the common sense of practitioners, but by replacing practical common sense with the theoretical knowledge of science. It is only by substituting the impersonal principles of science for the traditional principles of practice that evidence will replace ideology and the influence of subjective values be eliminated. And it is only by bringing this kind of educational theory to bear on educational practice that the instrumental value of practice can be assessed and more effective practices can be devised.

The 'practical' approach

This is the approach of David Evans and it informs much of the 'anti-positivist' thinking in curriculum theory and research. It thus underpins the 'illuminative' view of curriculum evaluation, 'process' models of curriculum design and the case study or 'naturalistic' approach to curriculum research.[7] As with the 'applied science' approach, educational theory is regarded as a form of inquiry aimed at improving the way in which practical decision-making is conducted. Where it differs is in the refusal to accept any restriction of the notion of 'theory' to empirical generalizations or any assimilation of the sphere of the 'practical' to the sphere of the 'technical'.

In this approach, to say that education is a practical activity is to concede that it is an open, reflective, indeterminate and complex form of human action which cannot be governed by theoretical principles or guided by technical rules. Thus, on this view, it is misguided to believe that educational theory can offer rigorous scientific knowledge by means of which practice can be regulated and controlled. All that it can offer is a form of knowledge that is always uncertain and incomplete but which can nevertheless provide a basis for making wise and prudent judgements about what, in some particular practical situation, ought to be done.

So construed, the aim of the 'practical approach' to educational theory is to feed practical wisdom. This it does by seeking to rehabilitate the art of 'deliberation' as a basis for making educationally defensible judgements about how to intervene in the complex on-going life of the classroom and the school. To this end, it offers practitioners interpretative theories which describe their practical situation in ways that are intended to help them to uncover their underlying values and to reveal the tacit and previously unacknowledged assumptions inherent in their work.

On this view then, educational practice is morally committed action: it is an essentially ethical activity guided by basic educational values rather than narrow instrumental or utilitarian concerns. But although educational practice always involves moral purposes and intentions, these are construed not as 'ends' to which practice is the technical means, but as educational commitments that can only be realized *in* and *through* practice. Practice, therefore, is not seen as an instrumental process serving fixed educational ends, but as a fluid activity in which the choice of both means and ends is guided by values and criteria immanent in the educational process itself: criteria which serve to distinguish practice which is educational from practice which is not, and good educational practice from practice which is indifferent or bad.

Given this view of practice, the purpose of theory is not to encourage conformity to a given tradition; still less is it to ensure conformity to scientific prescriptions. Rather, it is to encourage the disposition to make professional judgements that are enriched by educational principles and informed by a self-conscious understanding of the moral character of the educator's role. Theory relates to practice by enlightening practitioners; it aims to educate practitioners, deepen their insights and enliven their commitments so that they may see more deeply under the surface of their ideas and practices. So understood, educational theory is not an 'applied science', but a species of *Geisteswissenshriften* or 'moral science'.

The critical approach

This is the approach of Mary Jones. Although this approach has yet fully to penetrate the field of education, it is now beginning to attract interest, not least because it offers a way of reconstructing educational theory in which the insights of the 'common sense', the 'applied science' and the 'practical' approaches are acknowledged and preserved. Thus, although it shares the 'practical' insight that educational theory must be rooted in the common-sense beliefs and understandings of practitioners, it repudiates any suggestion that these beliefs and understandings cannot be casually determined or explained in objective terms. Similarly, although it shares the 'applied science' conviction that there may be causal factors operative in educational situations, it refuses to infer from this that educational theory can be produced without reference to the common-sense interpretations and understandings which practitioners employ.[8]

In attempting to reconcile the 'practical' concern with subjective understanding and the 'applied science' emphasis on objective explanation, the critical approach seeks to explain how objective factors can constrain the rationality of practitioners' beliefs and so distort their understanding of their practice. Thus, it takes as its subject matter the unquestioned beliefs, the self-evident truths and the common-sense understandings of practitioners in order to show how these may be the outcome of certain causal antecedent conditions – such as a certain form of social structure – of which practitioners may be ignorant but which may nevertheless operate to impede them in the rational pursuit of their educational task. It does so in the belief that the more practitioners know about the causal origins of their understandings and beliefs, the more will they be able to determine them in a rational way. Thus, the critical approach is not committed to any deterministic claim that because practice is causally determined it is, therefore, unalterable. On the contrary, it operates on the assumption that it is only by helping practitioners to become more self-conscious about the causal determinants of their beliefs and practices that they can bring them under greater rational self-control.

Thus, the aim of the critical approach is to increase the rational autonomy of practitioners. It pursues this aim by interpreting educational practice not simply as a moral practice but also as a social practice which is historically located, culturally embedded and, hence, always vulnerable to ideological distortion. Thus, educational practice is always interpreted as 'problematic', not in the sense that it gives rise to practical problems to which theoretical solutions can be applied, but in the sense that the purposes it serves, the social relationships it creates, the form of social life it helps to sustain, can all be critically reconsidered in terms of the way in which they either assist or impede genuine educational progress and change.

So understood, the critical approach, like the 'practical' approach, seeks to educate practitioners by promoting self-knowledge. What makes it distinctive is that it seeks to promote self-knowledge which not only 'enlightens' practitioners about their beliefs and understanding but also emancipates them from the irrational beliefs and misunderstandings that they have inherited from habit, tradition and ideology. To this end, it employs the method of ideology-critique: a method of critical self-reflection undertaken by practitioners in order to explore the irrationality of their common-sense beliefs and practices and to locate the source of this irrationality in the institutionalized context and forms of social life from which it emerged. By inviting practitioners to consider the rationality of their practices in a broad historical and social context, ideology-critique offers a means whereby distorted self-understandings can become transparent and so deprived of their power. Conceived as a process of ideology-critique, the relationship of theory and practice is not one of applying theory to practice; nor is it a matter of deriving theory from practice. Rather, by recovering self-reflection as a valid category of knowledge, the critical approach interprets theory and practice as mutually constitutive and dialectically related domains.

IV

In some ways the order in which I have placed these different views of theory and practice reflects the way in which the history of educational theorizing has evolved over the past century or so. In other ways, the categories I have adopted may be seen as a crude attempt to reassert the classical Aristotelian distinctions between the 'theoretical', 'productive' and 'practical' sciences, each with its own distinctive form of theorizing (*episteme*, *poietike* and *praxis*) and its own particular guiding dispositions (*theoria*, *technie*, *phronesis*). It would, however, be more accurate to say that the categories are intended to reflect Habermas's view that there are three general forms that the human and social sciences can take (empirical, interpretive, critical), each based on a different interpretation of the nature of human action and social life (instrumental, communicative, reflective) and each incorporating different preferences about the sort of practical purpose (or 'human interest') that social scientific theorizing should serve (technical, practical, emancipatory).[9] What, in effect, I have tried to argue is that different forms of educational theory are not only constitutive of different interpretations of the nature of educational practice; they incorporate different views about the practical purpose of educational theory as well.

Although the implications of this argument are, I suspect, far-reaching, my concluding comments are restricted to some brief observations about their implications for the study of education. At present, theoretical interest in the concepts of 'theory' and 'practice' is expressed in a way which does not fully acknowledge their mutual interdependence and so allows discussions of educational theory to proceed in virtual isolation from discussions about educational practice. Now it seems to me that this state of affairs is in part due to the fact that we persist in employing forms of educational inquiry in which the social and cultural context in which our contemporary understanding of the concepts of theory and practice is embedded can be more or less totally ignored. In doing this, we not only run the risk of concentrating our inquiries on one variation of the concept of educational theory to the exclusion of all others; we also expose ourselves to the danger of offering a spurious guarantee to that concept of theory which supports whatever concept of practice is dominant in a given cultural milieu. It is, I suspect, precisely because it appears to be conferring intellectual legitimacy on a concept of educational theory which is both historically contingent and culturally specific that this kind of educational theorizing is so frequently accused of serving to underpin, rather than expose, ideology.

What, in this chapter, I have tried to suggest is that educational theorizing will only remove suspicions about its ideological role when it becomes less concerned with discovering the 'logic' of educational theory and more concerned with recovering the logic of educational practice implicit in its own conceptual structures – a logic which educational theorists never explicitly defend but to which they always implicitly subscribe. It is only by exposing and articulating this logic that we can begin to acknowledge the preconceptions constitutive of our present understanding of educational theory and practice and of the relationship between the two. And it is only by rigorous criticism of these preconceptions that educational theorists can be confident that what they have to say about the practice of education is neither contaminated by ideological distortion nor corroded by intellectual complacency.

3   ADOPTING AN
EDUCATIONAL
PHILOSOPHY

> The majority of mankind are philosophers in so far as they
> engage in practical activity for, in their practical activity,
> there is implicitly contained a conception of the world, a
> philosophy . . . This conception of the world is mechanically
> imposed by one of the many social groups in which
> everyone is automatically involved from the moment of
> entry into the conscious world . . . Philosophy is not
> therefore, the intrusion into everyday life of an alien esoteric
> otiose knowledge but an essential dimension of essential
> human experience. Philosophy is renovating and making
> critical an already existing activity . . . it is the criticism and
> superarching of common-sense.[1]

I

The title of this chapter is more or less guaranteed to provoke feelings of
suspicion and unease. Is not 'educational philosophy' a prime example of the
kind of irrelevant theorizing that should be limited to the point of exclusion
by the coal face realities of actual school situations? Surely, so the argument
goes, the practical experience of teaching provides enough problems without
the 'intrusion' of this kind of 'alien, esoteric knowledge'.

As somebody who works mainly at the 'theory' end of the education business I find this kind of attitude hard to take – especially as I believe that it
contains more than a modicum of truth. However, I also believe that it con-
tributes to a misunderstanding that has impeded the development of proper
relationships between theorists and practitioners for a long time: the twin
illusions that some people 'theorize' about education but do not engage in any

practical activities, while others 'practise' education without engaging in any kind of theorizing. For this to stand any chance of being true, teaching would have to be some kind of mechanical behaviour performed by robot-like characters in a completely unthinking way. But teaching is not like that. Rather, it is a consciously performed activity that can only be made intelligible by reference to the quite complex ways of thinking in terms of which teachers understand what they are doing. And it is this 'way of thinking' that provides the theoretical background against which teachers explain and justify their actions, make decisions and resolve problems. Anybody engaged in teaching, then, must already possess some 'theory' which guides their practices and makes them intelligible.

As well as being self-consciously undertaken, teaching is also a social activity. To say this is to concede that the theory structuring the thoughts and practices of teachers is not something that they work out for themselves. Rather, it is a way of thinking and acting into which novice teachers are initiated and which is maintained through the routine, everyday social activities that occur in schools. It is, then, an inherited (or, in Gramsci's phrase, 'mechanically imposed') form of thought from which teachers derive their common-sense 'craft knowledge'. In short, it is what, within the teaching community, 'everybody knows'.

Teachers expose and articulate the theoretical understanding they have of their activities when they describe and explain such things as their choice of teaching methods, their attitudes to discipline and the selection of curriculum content. Now if further questions are asked about the adequacy of these descriptive accounts the discussion eventually becomes 'philosophical'. Questions arise about how the choice of teaching methods is justified, about the purposes that the selected curriculum content serves and – if this line of questioning is pushed far enough – about what precisely education is being taken to mean. In formulating answers to these questions, teachers are, in effect, revealing the cornerstones of the total conceptual structure within which their educational policies and practices are designed and executed. And to the extent that teachers try to justify their answers they try to demonstrate the rationality of the 'educational philosophies' in terms of which they operate.

'Educational philosophy', then, is not some kind of academic theory to which practising teachers may remain indifferent. It is more or less implicitly contained in the common-sense assumptions, values and beliefs underlying their everyday practical activities. Moreover, in so far as this common-sense thinking constitutes the basic patterns of thought in terms of which teachers make sense of what they are doing, it thereby defines the proper starting point for theorizing about their educational practice. This is not, of course, to say that teachers' common sense should provide the foundations on which an educational philosophy should be built. Nor does it entail accepting the educational beliefs and assumptions it incorporates. For the distinctive feature of common sense is not that its beliefs and assumptions *are* true but that it is a style of thinking in which the truth of these beliefs and assumptions is regarded as self-evident and taken for granted. What is commonsensical is *ipso facto* unquestionable and does not need to be justified. At the same time, however, because common-sense thinking is an inherited way of thinking, it always contains beliefs and assumptions that are the product of the customs, myths and prejudices of the past.[2]

The initial task, therefore, is not so much to decide which educational philosophy teachers should 'adopt' as to characterize the different 'philosophies' that have evolved out of the practical context of teaching and already underpin the conceptions of education that most teachers hold. What I want to suggest is that the various educational philosophies adopted by the teaching community to define and defend its practices cluster into two distinctive groups. These I intend to call 'traditional' and 'liberal progressive' but, in doing this, I want to emphasize that these labels should be treated with some caution. It would be a mistake to assume that any individual teacher's conception of what he or she is doing could be neatly located within one or other of these stances. 'Traditional' and 'liberal progressive' are simply 'ideal-type' constructs that are sufficiently coherent to allow the discernment of some more or less consistent strands in existing educational outlooks and actions.

II

The 'traditional' philosophy has its roots in pre-industrial society and remained dominant from classical times until the eighteenth century. Its view of society is aristocratic and it resonates with Plato's image of a society ruled by an elite group acting as the custodians of traditional values and universal truths. Since the primary function of education is to prepare an intellectual elite for the task of preserving their society's cultural heritage, the curriculum appropriate to this elite (but only this elite) is an academic curriculum in which classics, history, mathematics, grammar and literature predominate and 'modern' subjects such as science and technology are largely ignored. Rigorous selection is required to ensure that standards of 'academic excellence' are upheld and teachers are required to be authoritative masters of an academic discipline teaching in a formal, instructional and didactic way. Learning is systematic, disciplined and largely book-based. The assessment of learning is conducted through formal examinations designed to test the acquisition of abstract knowledge and the mastery of cognitive skills.

The 'liberal-progressive' educational philosophy emerged in the eighteenth and nineteenth centuries with the emergence of the liberal societies of Western Europe. Within this ideology, the main reproductive function of education is not cultural but political: to reproduce those forms of social life in which free and equal individuals can determine their own version of the 'good life' and collectively participate in formulating the common good of their society. Its view of society is thus egalitarian and it draws much of its inspiration from the political ideals espoused in Rousseau's *Social Contract* and the romantic and libertarian educational views expressed in his *Emile*.

Within a 'liberal-progressive' ideology, the aim of education is rational autonomy and freedom. Education is a process of rational development based on the common humanity of all rather than a process of cognitive acquisition based on the authoritative knowledge of an intellectual elite. For this reason,

Table 3.1   Traditional and liberal-progressive educational philosophies

	Traditional	*Liberal progressive*
Political perspective	Conservative	Liberal/communitarian
View of society	Elitist	Egalitarian
Guiding educational slogan	'Academic excellence'	'Learning from experience'
Canonical texts	Plato's *Republic*	Rousseau's *Emile*
Types of schools	Grammar schools	Community schools
Classroom organization	Rigid grouping of pupils on the basis of intellectual ability	Flexible grouping of pupils on the basis of needs and interests
Curriculum content	Subject-centred: rigid subject differentiation	Child-centred: weak subject differentiation
Curriculum knowledge	Objective knowledge	Subjective knowledge
Teacher's role	Expert, transmitting cultural heritage	Facilitator, enabling pupils to learn from personal learning
Teaching methods	Formal instruction	'Discovery' methods
Assessment procedures	Traditional examinations to test the acquisition of knowledge	Informal evaluations of qualitative developments in pupils' understanding

the curriculum reflects pupils' developmental needs rather than society's culture and its content is largely defined on the basis of pupils' needs and interests. Academic subjects have a very limited curriculum role and the passive transmission of society's knowledge is always subordinate to the active development of the pupil's understanding. The teacher is primarily a guide rather than an instructor and teaching is largely a matter of stimulating pupils' natural curiosity and facilitating their own inquiries.

It may be useful to set out these two educational philosophies in a diagrammatic form, as in Table 3.1.

It is important to make three related points about the way in which these educational philosophies are usually presented and described. First, the fact that they are often analysed in an ahistorical way should not obscure the fact that each is the product of a particular historical period and emerged in response to new social circumstances and changing cultural conditions. Second, the fact that these educational philosophies have been portrayed as mutually exclusive should not be allowed to obscure the extent to which, in practice, they merge and overlap. Nor should the fact that they have been presented as conflicting philosophies be allowed to obscure how they share some important similarities. Both, for example, see education as intrinsically concerned with developing pupils' capabilities for rational autonomous thought. Of course, what, within the two perspectives, concepts like 'rational thought' mean and the reasons why 'autonomy' is regarded as an education goal will be very different. Within the traditional philosophy, for example, it is often argued that the initiation into a predetermined set of academic disciplines is an

essential prerequisite to achieving intellectual development and rational autonomy. Within the progressive philosophy, however, because greater emphasis
is given to the nature of the pupil as an already active thinking individual, it is
argued that the future autonomy of pupils can only be effectively pursued by
assisting them to conduct their present thinking in more coherent and intelligent ways.

As well as this mutual concern with rational autonomous thought, there is
another common presumption that should not be overlooked: the shared
belief that educational practices need to be rationally justified and defended.
In the very process of elaborating their arguments about educational purposes,
traditional and liberal-progressive philosophies both endorse the belief that
education must have some intrinsic purpose and value. Indeed, it is only
because of the common conviction that educational practices always imply
some such commitment that teachers ever feel it necessary to indulge in
'philosophical' discussions about what in substantial terms the nature of this
value may be. If teachers did not perceive any intrinsic purpose to education,
if, that is, they employed no distinctively educational criteria, they could not
even identify an educative practice apart from one that sought, say, to indoc-
trinate or brainwash pupils. In short, without some 'educational philosophy',
teachers' conceptions of themselves as educators would disappear.

III

I have drawn attention to these similarities not to create the impression that
there are no important differences between traditional and liberal-progressive
philosophies, but to demonstrate how, to the extent that they both seek to
provide rational foundations for their respective conceptions of education,
they both invite critical analysis and assessment. Assessing their coherence
and intellectual order is a difficult and important task for any self-critical
teacher to undertake. But more difficult still is the task of relating *either* of
these educational philosophies to the realities of educational practice. For the
sad truth is that the promises and expectations that both these philosophies
offer rarely materialize. Look into any classroom and it is entirely probable
that what is going on will bear little resemblance to the educational philosophy of the teachers or the school. In saying this, I do not just have in mind
those familiar discrepancies between the prescriptions that flow from any
'official' educational philosophy and the sort of educational practices actually
being pursued. What I am really referring to are the contradictions that exist
between what teachers and schools *think* and *say* that they are doing and what
they *are* doing. In schools and other educational institutions there is always a
world of difference between teachers' beliefs about their educational practices
and those practices themselves.

At this point let me try to provide a couple of examples of the sort of
disconnections that I have in mind. The belief that pupils should 'learn
through interest' is a postulate of the liberal-progressive philosophy that has
attracted considerable support. In adopting this idea, however, teachers soon
discover that what they want pupils to learn and what interests pupils are two

very different things. Almost immediately, therefore, the very meaning of the 'teaching through interest' idea is reinterpreted so as to refer to the practice of presenting teacher-approved subject matter in 'an interesting way'. So, for example, in attempting to get pupils to learn biology 'through interest' a teacher may make use of their interest in animals. But, clearly, in doing this he is not making biology interesting; whatever 'interest' the pupils may have in biology derives solely from its being a means to their interest in animals. The question of whether the pupils are interested in biology or whether biology is itself interesting does not even arise.

Nobody should be under any illusion that these kind of distortions are confined to attempts to adopt a liberal-progressive educational philosophy; they also pervade the practices of teachers favouring a more traditional approach. Take, for example, those adherents to traditional philosophies who explain and justify the teaching of history by pointing to its importance in developing a distinctive way of thinking about contemporary culture and society. Now, in practice, history is not usually taught as a distinctive way of thinking but as a series of dates, events and facts that pupils can do little with except rote-learn and memorize. Although many teachers seem to believe that by teaching history in this way they are applying a traditional 'subject-centred' philosophy, nothing could be further from the truth. Far from being taught to learn the process of historical thinking, pupils are simply being induced to acquire the products of the historical thinking of others. Moreover, this general strategy of presenting the various academic disciplines as inert bodies of knowledge infects, as far as I can see, all subject-teaching. Science, literature, geography and the rest are taught not as distinctive modes of thinking and understanding but as a more or less monotonous diet of disjointed facts which pupils have to digest and regurgitate if they are to stand any chance of success.

Why is this so? Why do thoughtful and intelligent teachers find it so difficult to bring their practices into line with their beliefs and ideas? What is it that causes teachers' educational ideas to become distorted and why are their attempts to pursue more coherent and rational educational practices so easily frustrated?

Clues to how these questions may be answered are not hard to find. One of the enduring features of the deschooling rhetoric of the early 1970s is the insight that the activities of schools, irrespective of the kind of educational philosophy that they endorse, are firmly governed by a view of education which is neither 'traditional' nor 'liberal progressive', which is never officially formulated or defended and, hence, which never needs to produce any rational account of its merits. Schools are constrained to act in this way because, as well as being educational institutions, they are also social institutions. And, as such, they have an internal logic which unavoidably impels them towards a 'hidden' curriculum that inculcates predominant moral, social and political values.[3] Hence, teachers find it difficult to practise what they preach not because of any failings or weaknesses on their part, but because schools must reflect the purposes and pressures of contemporary society. In consequence, the claims of teachers to be pursuing educative policies or practices, whether traditional or progressive, are often no more than contrived rationalizations designed to make these purposes and pressures bearable. The sheer ingenuity displayed by schools in absorbing, like cotton wool, any new ideas while remaining basically unchanged, is not only indicative of the power of the social forces that shape educational institutions; it also indicates how the problem of 'adopting an educational philosophy' is more the province of political and social philosophy than any philosopher's 'philosophy of education'. But, more than this, it reveals how any philosophical thinking about education is always a matter of grasping, through reflective self-critical thought, the goals and style of society and the role of education in achieving this goal and maintaining this style. It is precisely because the goals and styles of contemporary society are incompatible with any rational educational philosophy that a teacher who tries to practise the belief that education should have goals he can justify and a style he can accept will have to stand against a current that will, in all probability, overwhelm him. Let me elaborate.

What is basic to most schools is their domination by a sort of ladder mentality. The skills pupils learn at primary school are taught because they are needed in secondary schools. The subjects in the secondary school curriculum have to be learned in order to get the qualifications required for higher education which itself is a necessary prerequisite for obtaining a good job. Now what needs to be emphasized is how none of the particular steps on this ladder seems to have any intrinsic educational value. Education is perceived as having only an instrumental value as a means to something other than education itself. Perceived in this way, education is not even remotely concerned with the development of rational autonomy and intellectual freedom. It is only concerned with fitting people with the attitudes and skills necessary to be successful in a society in which this kind of instrumental rationality is endemic.

Teachers' philosophies, because they rarely regard education as an instrumental means to some non-educational end, do not fit well into this kind of society. Yet, because we are so imbued with the ethos of our age, the idea that education is a means to the satisfaction of material needs seems obvious to all. It is this all-pervading instrumental mentality that makes the proper implementation of any coherent educational philosophy all but impossible. The pressure to equip pupils with the values and qualifications necessary for them to fit into this way of life is almost irresistible. Even the most resolute teachers, not wanting their pupils to come to grief, may have to skip their education in order to ensure their market value. And they will quickly realize that to try to answer questions about the curriculum in terms of its educational value and purpose will not convince politicians or parents, who, by and large, demand instrumental answers in terms of the functions education performs as a means to something else. To politicians, education is about providing an adequate labour force and raising the gross national product; to parents it is about acquiring qualifications, status and a career. And to those pupils who can pick up the rules of the game, education soon becomes a matter of gaining stars, points and marks and acquiring the certificates and diplomas that will lead to a good job. It is, above all, because teachers' educational philosophies are incompatible with the role that schools have been given in our society that their realization is all but impossible. Adopting an educational philosophy is so difficult because it demands all that society tends to deny.

IV

In conclusion, let me give a final glance both ways – at what I am for and what I am against. What I am *against* is the instrumental use of schools for purposes other than educational ones. When this happens the pupils' ability to think rationally and critically is the price they have to pay for the preservation of some dubious social values. What I am *for* is the development of educational practices in which the education of pupils is allowed to count. What I am *for* is recognizing that education does not merely have a social utility or a productive usefulness and that attempts to characterize it in these terms only succeed in undermining and degrading it.

But quite apart from what I'm for and against, the important point at issue seems to be this. All teachers are, at some time or other, faced with the personal dilemma of deciding whether to be committed to their educative task or whether to play their role, advance their prospects and leave the commitment to somebody else. It is one thing to acquire a stock of sophisticated teaching competencies and master the intricacies of modern technological aids; it is quite another to have the educational character of teaching as an ultimate professional concern. Within contemporary society, this kind of concern is often treated as a major weakness, and actually to practise the educational philosophies that schools so often say are desirable is to risk being thought a crank, a fool or, at best, somebody who has no interest in climbing up the ladder of his chosen profession. But teaching is only a genuine profession to the extent that its members maintain the right to make independent judgements free from external coercion and pressures. It is precisely this feature of professionalism which ensures that teachers are not the paid agents of society whose responsibilities and decisions are controlled by some political masters. In default of protecting their educational philosophies, teachers quickly become the instrument of non-professional non-educational pressures. Resisting these pressures – not allowing them to distort or frustrate genuine educational ideas – is impossibly difficult. But there is a world of difference between doing something very difficult and doing something that does not make any sense. Adopting an educational philosophy is very difficult.

4 WHAT IS AN

EDUCATIONAL

PRACTICE?

> A practice . . . is never just a set of technical skills . . . What
> is distinctive of a practice is in part the way in which
> conceptions of the relevant goods and ends which the
> technical skills serve – and every practice does require the
> exercise of technical skills – are transformed and enriched by
> those extensions of human powers and by that regard for its
> own internal goods which are partially definitive of each
> particular practice.[1]

I

It has become rather fashionable these days to extol the virtues of educational
practice. Teacher education should be more firmly based on it, educational
theorizing should be made more relevant to it and teacher educators should
have more experience of it. Given this state of affairs, it is surprising to find
that educational philosophers who willingly argue about the meaning of 'educational theory' seem rather reluctant to discuss how the concept of 'educational practice' ought to be understood.[2] Indeed, it seems to be assumed that
the meaning of 'educational practice' is so straightforward and clear that we
can safely rely on our common-sense understanding when we use the term in
educational discussions and debates. The possibility that our common sense
may, in this instance, be in need of philosophical examination does not seem
to have been seriously considered or explored.

But suppose it were the case that our common-sense understanding of educational practice was radically ambiguous and incoherent. Suppose, further,
that the defects in our concept of educational practice not only predate

modern forms of educational theorizing, but actually paved the way for their evolution and growth. If this were the case, if, that is, our concept of educational theory *and* our concept of educational practice both emanated from the same dubious historical source, then we could expect certain difficulties to arise. We could, for example, expect to find that all our efforts to make educational theory 'practically relevant' were constantly breaking down. Despite our best intentions, the 'gap' between theory and practice would stubbornly remain. We could also expect to find that any philosophical inquiry into the meaning of 'educational practice' which simply concentrated on how this concept is now used would fail to detect the inherited weaknesses which our modern concept contained. Indeed, a philosophy of education committed to this kind of ahistorical conceptual analysis would offer nothing but an empty silence towards the numerous philosophical puzzles to which our ambiguous and incoherent understanding of educational practice inevitably gave rise.

The argument of this chapter is that these suppositions are largely true and hence that our contemporary concept of educational practice is the end-product of a historical process through which an older, more comprehensive and more coherent concept has been gradually transformed and changed. Given this thesis, it is not my intention to treat the title of this chapter as an invitation to analyse the ways in which the concept of educational practice is presently understood. On the contrary, I intend to regard it as an open invitation to allow the history of the concept to expose possibilities of meaning which are very different from those now encountered in contemporary use.

In order to respond to the question in this way, I have set myself three specific tasks. The first is to show why attempts to analyse the concept of 'practice' which focus on its relationship to 'theory' fail to furnish us with a satisfactory understanding of what an educational practice is. The second is to argue that this failure is in part due to the absence of any historical exegesis of the concept of 'practice' – a state of affairs which itself exemplifies the common belief that concepts can be philosophically analysed apart from their history. The third is to show that once we are prepared to give historical depth to philosophical analysis, it becomes possible to spell out a core concept of practice which not only illuminates some of the incoherences in our present conception of educational practice but also offers a more satisfactory understanding of why it is that education is understood as a practice at all.

II

In education, as elsewhere, the notion of 'practice' is used in different and, sometimes, incompatible ways. It is used, for example, to refer both to an activity undertaken in order to acquire certain capacities and skills ('teaching practice') and to an activity which demonstrates that these competences and skills have already been acquired ('good practice'). Normally, this ambiguity does not give rise to confusion: the context in which the notion occurs is sufficient to indicate the particular way it is being used.

What do give rise to some confusions, however, are those occasions when the concept of 'practice' is understood in terms of its relationship to theory.

The most common way of understanding this relationship is, of course, as one of opposition. On this view, 'practice' is everything that 'theory' is not. 'Theory' is concerned with universal, context-free generalizations; 'practice' with particular context-dependent instances. 'Theory' deals with abstract ideas; 'practice' with concrete realities. Theorizing is largely immune from the pressures of time; practice is responsive to the contingent demands of everyday life. Solutions to theoretical problems are found in knowing something; practical problems can only be solved by doing something. As one exponent of this 'oppositional' view puts it, 'a theoretical problem does not specify any occasion or situation in which it must be solved . . . but a practical problem can only be solved by taking action in a certain situation at a certain time'.[3]

When applied to the field of education, however, this view of practice is always unsatisfactory. For example, certain educational problems (What should I teach? What should I include in the curriculum?) are clearly 'practical' in the sense that they are problems about what to do. At the same time, however, they are 'general' rather than 'particular', 'abstract' rather than 'concrete', and relatively 'context-free'. Conversely, there are many educational problems that are 'specific', 'immediate' and 'context-dependent' (what are the major impediments in this school to teaching GCSE?) even though they are 'theoretical' in the sense that they are requests for knowledge rather than action. The situation is further complicated by the fact that there are numerous educational situations in which the practical point at issue is what to do about some theoretical claim (should I group pupils on the assumption that claims about innate differences in intelligence are true?). In such cases, the practical situation may call for immediate action based on a timeless question that has been debated 'in theory' since the time of Plato.

Thus, the general weakness of this 'oppositional' view is that it generates criteria for 'practice' which, when applied to the notion of an *educational* practice, exclude too much. By seeing 'theory' and 'practice' as mutually exclusive and diametrically opposed concepts, it tends to neglect these aspects of educational practice which are not constrained by criteria of immediacy, particularity, context-dependency and the like. And, by emphasizing the difference between knowledge and action, it tends to ignore the essential role in educational practice that theoretical generalizations and abstract ideas can play. In short, by making the twin assumptions that all practice is non-theoretical and all theory is non-practical, this approach always underestimates the extent to which those who engage in educational practices have to reflect upon, and hence theorize about, what, in general, they are trying to do.

The predictable reaction to these deficiencies has been the emergence of various accounts of educational practice which focus on its dependence on, rather than its opposition to, theory. Drawing on familiar philosophical arguments about the indispensability of conception schemes or the role of 'paradigms' in everyday life,[4] these analyses emphasize that, since all practice presupposes a more or less coherent set of assumptions and beliefs, it is, to this extent, always guided by a framework of theory. Thus, on this view, all practice, like all observation, is 'theory-laden'. 'Practice' is not opposed to theory, but is itself governed by an implicit theoretical framework which structures and guides the activities of those engaged in practical pursuits.

It follows from this kind of analysis that all practice is theory-laden and this will be just as true for the most simple practice (e.g. asking a pupil a question) as for those more complex cases in which the dependence on theory is more explicit and overt (e.g. using microcomputers to implement Skinnerian principles of learning). It thus needs to be emphasized that, on this account, the notion of 'theory-guided practice' can be used in two quite different ways. In the first place, it can be used to make the point that all practice necessarily presupposes a conceptual framework. But, secondly, it may also be used to describe those occasions when practitioners appropriate externally produced theory to guide them in their practical pursuits.

Just as the problem with the oppositional view of educational practice is that it excludes too much, so the general problem with the 'theory-guided' view is that it excludes too little. Indeed, on this view, educational practice can be guided by a 'theory' that is nothing other than tacit, implicit and unarticulated common sense as well as the 'theory' that is produced through systematic disciplined inquiry. But the most important difficulty with this view is that it does not adequately recognize that educational practice can never be guided by theory alone. This is so because 'theory', whether implicit and tacit or explicit and overt, is always a set of general beliefs, while 'practice' always involves taking action in a particular situation. Although practice may be guided by some implicit theoretical principles about what, in general, ought to be done, the decision to invoke or apply such principles in any particular situation cannot itself be guided or determined by theoretical beliefs. For this would entail an infinite regress of first order theoretical precepts (about what, in general, ought to be done) guided by second order meta-theoretical precepts (about if and when to apply first order theoretical precepts) and so on. Because practitioners are not subject to this infinite regress, their judgements about the applicability of general principles to particular situations cannot themselves be determined by theoretical principles or rules.

If educational practice cannot be reduced to a form of theorizing, can educational theorizing be reduced to a form of practice? One of the most influential attempts to pursue this line of thought is Gilbert Ryle's well-known attempt to assert the autonomy of practice.[5] Ryle developed his argument by showing that since one cannot 'know that' something is the case unless one already 'knows how' to do a vast number of things, 'know-how' is a concept logically prior to 'know-that'.[6] This not only entails that 'practice is not the step-child of theory'[7] but quite the reverse; 'efficient practice precedes the theory of it'.[8] Indeed, Ryle concluded that theorizing is itself a form of practice, requiring skill, competence and know-how of various kinds. ('Theorising is one practice among others and is itself intelligently or stupidly conducted'[9]).

The fact that Ryle is so effective in refuting the idea that practice is guided by some prior act of theorizing should not conceal how, by equating practice to 'knowing how' to perform various operations or skills, he employs it in a way that is more narrow and restricted than might first appear.[10] Nor should it cause us to forget that an educational practice always involves much more than 'knowing how' to do something in this Rylean sense. For a definitive feature of an *educational* practice is that it is an ethical activity undertaken in pursuit of educationally worthwhile ends. Moreover, as Professor Peters has so frequently pointed out, these ends are not some independently determined 'good' to which educational practice is the instrumental means. Rather they define the rules of conduct, or, in Peters's phrase, the 'principles of procedure' which constitute a practice as an educational practice and justify its description in these terms.[11]

To engage in an educational practice it is thus never sufficient (though it is always necessary) to 'know how' to do a variety of things. We can, for example, consistently assert that a certain teaching method is competently and skilfully performed (e.g. the techniques of behaviour modification) yet deny that it is an educational practice. To make this assertion is to claim not that this form of teaching is ineffective but that it is incompatible with those ethical principles by which any educational practice must be informed. This is not to say that, in order to engage in an educational practice, these ethical principles need to be translated into a set of codified rules which can then be used to guide practice in an educationally worthwhile direction. It is simply to point out that the educational character of any practice can only be made intelligible by reference to an ethical disposition to proceed according to some more or less tacit understanding of what it is to act educationally. Where this disposition is present, a practitioner may, irrespective of his 'know-how' or skill, practise in an educational way. But where it is absent, a practitioner who 'knows how' to practise, in a Rylean sense, will be quite incapable of practising in an educational sense at all.

The simple lesson of the argument so far is that the three accounts of practice I have identified are all inadequate for determining how the concept of educational practice ought to be understood. One conclusion that could be inferred is that it reinforces the suspicion that a question like 'what is an educational practice?' is wholly misconceived. 'Practice' has such a plethora of meaning that the search for criteria which can provide our concept of educational practice with some kind of definitive meaning presupposes that it has a unity and simplicity which it patently does not.

Another, less obvious, conclusion may be that it is not the question that is misconceived but our presumptions about how it is to be answered. It may be plausible to suggest that the reason why these accounts of practice do not enable us to make our concept of an educational practice more intelligible is not that they are false. It may well be that the three features of a practice to which they draw attention (its opposition to theory, its dependence on theory, its independence of theory) are all necessary features of an educational practice as well. But by accentuating only one of these features to the exclusion of the others, each of these different accounts may only be offering an incomplete, one-sided, version of what an educational practice may be. Once they are looked at in this way, these accounts of practice no longer appear as three incompatible alternatives from which we have to choose. They can instead be seen to be three incomplete analyses of a practice, each of which is limited by two false assumptions.

The first of these is that the meaning of practice can only be determined by clarifying how it relates to theory, so that to understand what a practice is, it is always necessary to understand this relationship. The second is that 'practice' is a stable and static concept, so that in any philosophical analysis of its meaning, its history will only be of incidental or antiquarian interest. But once these two assumptions are challenged, it becomes possible to interpret the criteria of 'practice' provided by each of these analyses in a very different way. It becomes plausible to interpret them not as mutually exclusive criteria, but as three essential features of a historically prior concept of practice for which problems about its relationship to theory do not arise.

To interpret matters in this way is thus to suggest that the various criteria surrounding our present concept of practice are nothing other than the fragmented relics of a previous concept of practice which, though it can no longer find adequate expression, nevertheless continues to convey something of its original meaning and assert something of its original form. It is also to suggest that we ought to be able to produce a historical reconstruction of this concept which will enable us to clarify some of the ambiguity surrounding its contemporary meaning and use. But is it appropriate to try and answer a question like 'what is an educational practice?' in this way? Much of the contemporary philosophy of education asserts that it is not. Indeed, the intellectual predilections now cultivated by the academic study of education encourage us to believe that philosophical analysis is one thing and the history of ideas is something else. But are we right to construe the relationship between the philosophy and the history of education in this way? To this question I now, albeit briefly, wish to turn.

III

An ancient statue of a Roman god will have a history. It is a history of a stable and unchanging object which has continued to exhibit the same essential features over time. As such, it reminds us of the time and place in which it was produced and so helps us to understand the particular culture and form of social life which it expresses and represents. The concepts we use to describe this statue will also have histories. But the history of concepts like 'religious', or 'god', is not the history of an unchanging object displaying the same essential features throughout time. Concepts are not kept in museums to remind us of the particular form of life in which they have their origins or roots. They continue to be used and, in continuing to be used, they change. How concepts like 'religious' and 'god' are used at any given time and place will vary as social life varies. Conversely, as changes in social life occur so changes in the meaning of concepts will occur as well.[12]

The simple reason why this is so is that conceptual structures and social structures are neither separable nor distinct.[13] Concepts are socially embedded and a form of social life is partially constituted by concepts. So, for example, the differences between the ancient Greek concepts of 'democracy', 'citizen' and 'justice' and the contemporary English usages of these terms signifies not simply a linguistic difference, but a difference between two forms of social life.

Thus, one important way of understanding the concept of 'practice' available to any given historical period would be to uncover the rules governing its use in language and social life. Similarly, one important way of identifying changes that are occurring in our own culture may be by noting changes in the way that the concept of 'practice' is now being used.

The fact that conceptual change and social change are two elements in one essentially dialectical process should not encourage us to assume that this process can somehow occur without direct human intervention. Nor, in particular, should it cause us to overlook the important part that philosophical inquiry can play in influencing this process. For if a philosophical analysis can succeed in revealing that the way in which a concept is being used is in need of major modification or revision, then it may thereby assist in the process of changing its everyday interpretation and use. Philosophical analysis of what concepts mean and changing social life are thus not necessarily independent tasks. Indeed, it may well be that the role now played by the concept of practice in social life is partially owing to the way in which it has been analysed by philosophers in some previous era.[14]

To see the history of the concept of practice in these terms is thus to recognize the limitations of any philosophical inquiry which restricts itself to analysing that version of the concept which our own cultural milieu happens to provide. It is also to concede that the only sure antidote to this kind of conceptual parochialism is to bring our own contemporary understanding of the concept of practice face to face with a historical account of how it has been understood in the past. Unless we are prepared to allow the history of the concept of practice to break down our present-day preconceptions in this way, then we may be deprived of important clues for detecting possible confusions and distortions in the way the concept is now used.

Interpreted as a request for historical intelligibility (rather than an analysis of contemporary usage), the question 'what is an educational practice?' presages a form of inquiry committed to the combined tasks of historical reconstruction and philosophical critique. What we could expect such an inquiry to reveal is that the concept of an educational practice is largely explicable in terms of four characteristic historical features. The first is that our present concept of an educational practice has its origins within the conceptual structures of a form of life which has long since disappeared and, hence, that it can only be made fully intelligible by understanding it as a survival from a social context very different from our own.

The second is that, in this transition from one social context to another, what it means to talk of education as a practice will have changed. Thus, we should be prepared to find that, in the transition from the context in which it was originally at home to our own contemporary culture, an educational practice became something other than it once was. But what, thirdly, we should also expect to find, is that such changes in the concept will not be so complete as to eradicate its original meaning or detach it totally from its historical roots. So it should be unsurprising to discover that, as any new conceptions of an educational practice emerge, fragments of an older concept will continue to assert themselves and break through. The history of concepts is one of continuity as well as change.

What, finally, we would expect a full-length history of the concept of an educational practice to reveal are those occasions where changes to its meaning may have been assisted by abstract philosophical ideas about the nature of education itself. It is only by first appreciating the extent to which our present concept of an educational practice relies on the educational ideas and arguments of our philosophical ancestors that we can critically assess the extent to which this present-day concept can be philosophically vindicated and sustained.

The question 'what is an educational practice?' can now be recast in the following more precise and more answerable form: can we discover a historically specific concept of practice which enables us to reconcile the seemingly irreconcilable range of criteria governing its present use? Can we recover from history a core concept of practice which is more compelling for education than our own? The answer I intend to provide is that we can, and that it turns out to be the classical concept of practice which has always exercised a decisive influence on education and which has only been finally discarded in our own modern times. This concept of practice owes much to the philosophy of Aristotle. It was he who initiated the search for the forms of knowledge and rationality appropriate to practical action. And it is only through a historical understanding of his account of practice that we shall be able to appreciate why it is that education is now construed as a practice at all.

IV

Although the Greek word *praxis* has a meaning roughly corresponding to our term 'practice', the conceptual structures within which it has its proper place are very different from our own. For, in its classical context, 'practice' referred to a distinctive way of life – the *bios praktikos* – a life devoted to right living through the pursuit of the human good. It was distinguishable from a life devoted to *theoria* (*bios theoretikos*) – the contemplative way of life of the philosopher or the scientist – in terms of both its end and the means of pursuing this end.[15]

Thus, the Greek distinction between theory and practice has very little to do with the way in which the distinction is now drawn. It is not a distinction between knowledge and action, thinking and doing, 'knowing that' and 'knowing how'. Rather, it is a way of articulating two different forms of socially embedded human activities, each with its own intellectual commitments and its own moral demands. It is thus unsurprising to find that in their discussions about *theoria* and *praxis*, the Greeks rarely found it necessary to discuss the relationship between the two. For them, the modern philosophical problem of whether theory and practice are, or are not, independent of each other would have made little sense.[16]

A problem about practice to which the Greeks did attach philosophical importance was that of clarifying the forms of knowledge and rationality appropriate to practical thought and action. One way of reading the *Nichomachean Ethics* is as a brilliant attempt to resolve this problem by elucidating the epistemological presuppositions of *praxis*. In doing this, Aristotle not only opened up that tradition of 'practical philosophy' which henceforth was to provide the *bios praktikos* with its major source of theoretical expression and support. He also articulated a range of conceptual distinctions which now enable us to distinguish beliefs about 'practice' which belong to this tradition from beliefs which do not.

The most important of these distinctions is not between theory and practice but between two forms of human action – *praxis* and *poiesis* – a distinction which can only be rendered in English by our much less precise notions of 'doing something' and 'making something'. *Poiesis* – 'making action' – is action whose end is to bring some specific product or artefact into existence. Because the end of *poiesis* is an object which is known prior to action, it is guided by a form of knowledge which Aristotle called *techne* – what we would now call technical knowledge or expertise. *Poiesis* is thus a species of rule-following action. It is what Weber was to call 'purposive-rational' action and what we would call instrumental action. For Aristotle and the Greeks, the activities of shipbuilders, craftsmen and artisans were paradigm cases of *poiesis* guided by *techne*.

Although 'practice' (*praxis*) is also action directed towards the achievement of some end, it differs from *poiesis* in several crucial respects. In the first place, the end of a practice is not to produce an object or artefact but to realize some morally worthwhile 'good'. But, second, practice is not a neutral instrument by means of which this 'good' can be produced. The 'good' for the sake of which a practice is pursued cannot be 'made', it can only be 'done'. 'Practice' is a form of 'doing action' precisely because its end can only be realized through action and can only exist in the action itself.

Thus, third, practice can never be understood as a form of technical expertise designed to achieve some externally related end. Nor can these ends be specified in advance of engaging in a practice. Indeed, *praxis* is different from *poiesis* precisely because discernment of the 'good' which constitutes its end is inseparable from a discernment of its mode of expression. 'Practice' is thus what we would call morally informed or morally committed action. Within the Aristotelian tradition all ethical and political activities were regarded as forms of practice. And so too, of course, was education.

Another way in which practice differs from *poiesis* is that its ends are neither immutable nor fixed. Instead, they are constantly revised as the 'goods' intrinsic to practice are progressively pursued. Thus, while it is always possible, and frequently desirable, to produce a theoretical specification of what the ends of *poiesis* should be, the ends of practice cannot be determined in this way. Rather, what they are at any given time can only be made intelligible in terms of the inherited and largely unarticulated body of practical knowledge which constitutes the tradition within which the good intrinsic to a practice is enshrined. To practise is thus never a matter of individuals accepting and implementing some rational account of what the 'aims' of their practice should be. It is always a matter of being initiated into the knowledge, under-standings and beliefs[17] bequeathed by that tradition through which the practice has been conveyed to us in its present shape.[18]

To 'practise', then, is always to act within a tradition, and it is only by submitting to its authority that practitioners can begin to acquire the practical knowledge and standards of excellence by means of which their own practical competence can be judged.[19] But the authoritative nature of a tradition does not make it immune to criticism. The practical knowledge made available through tradition is not mechanically or passively reproduced: it is constantly being reinterpreted and revised through dialogue and discussion about how to pursue the practical goods which constitute the tradition.[20] It is precisely because it embodies this process of critical reconstruction that a tradition evolves and changes rather than remains static or fixed. When the ethical aims of a practice are officially deemed to be either uncontentious or impervious to rational discussion, the notions of practical knowledge and tradition will tend to be used in a wholly negative way.[21]

Rational discussion about how the ethical ends of a practice were to be interpreted and pursued was what Aristotle took 'practical philosophy' to be all about.[22] It is the 'science' which seeks to raise the practical knowledge embedded in tradition to the level of reflective awareness and, through critical argument, to correct and transcend the limitations of what within this tradition has hitherto been thought, said and done. Thus the persistence, within this kind of practical philosophy, of incommensurable historical 'philosophies' about what the aims of a practice should be is neither a sign of its irrationality nor a source of intellectual embarrassment. On the contrary, it is the continuing presence of contesting philosophical viewpoints that provides the oppositional tension essential for critical thinking to perform its transforming role. Once deprived of this critical tension, 'practical philosophy' will quickly degenerate into a chronologically arranged catalogue of philosophical creeds and its relationship to practice will become increasingly difficult to discern.

Although, for Aristotle, practical philosophy is a 'science', it is not a 'theoretical science' devoted to pursuing *a priori* knowledge of the 'good' or a purely intellectual understanding of what, morally, ought to be done. Nor is it a 'productive science' yielding ethically neutral knowledge of effective skills and techniques. Rather, it is a 'practical science' yielding knowledge of how to promote the good through morally right action. But although practical philosophy offers ethical generalizations about the ends of a practice and how they ought to be pursued, this kind of knowledge is never sufficient to determine what a practitioner ought to do. In the first place, such knowledge is always imprecise: it merely states the general directions that practical action ought to take. Second, while practical philosophy can only provide general guidance, practice is itself always particular and has to take account of the changing conditions under which it has to operate. For these reasons practical philosophy cannot be used simply as a source of theoretical statements from which practical implications can be logically informed. Nor are the practical principles supplied by practical philosophy applicable as they stand. What any ethical principle means always has to be understood in terms of its relevance to a particular situation, just as the meaning of a particular situation always has to be understood in terms of the relevant ethical principles that are being applied. Understanding and applying ethical principles are thus not two separate processes but mutually constitutive elements in the continuous dialectical reconstruction of knowledge and action.

It follows from this that 'practical philosophy' is not concerned to characterize or specify the 'ends' of moral activities separately from the 'means of their realization'. Specific ethical ends (such as freedom and equality) are themselves simply the 'means' to the 'good' which is the all-embracing ultimate end of *praxis*. But of course the notion of the 'good' does not specify some fixed terminal end-point. What it specifies are those modes of ethical conduct which constitute the appropriate means for pursuing this end. 'Means' are thus nothing other than concrete ways of specifying how the notion of the 'good' is being understood, just as an understanding of the 'good' is nothing other than an abstract way of specifying the particular means by which it is to be enacted and realized.

Since the ends of a practice always remain indeterminate and cannot be fixed in advance, it always requires a form of reasoning in which choice, deliberation and practical judgement play a crucial role. This form of reasoning is, for Aristotle, distinguishable from technical forms of reasoning by virtue of its overall purpose and the structure of reasoning it employs.

The overall purpose of technical reasoning is to consider the relative effectiveness of action as a means to some known end – as, for example, when a teacher has to decide between 'phonic' and 'whole-word' approaches to the teaching of reading solely on the basis of their effectiveness in producing some specific outcome. By contrast, the overall purpose of practical reasoning is to decide what to do when faced with competing and, perhaps, conflicting moral ideals. Practical reasoning is thus most clearly exemplified in the thoughts and actions of those faced with a moral conflict or a moral dilemma. It is required, for example, when an individual has to decide whether to put loyalty to a friend before patriotic duty, or when a teacher has to decide whether it is educationally more desirable to segregate pupils on the basis of their ability or to adopt a 'mixed ability' approach. More generally, practical reasoning is required when practitioners have to decide on a course of action where it may only be possible to respect one value at the expense of another. In such cases, a practitioner cannot resort to a form of reasoning which relies on technical calculations to determine what course of action is correct. Practical reasoning is not a method for determining *how* to do something, but for deciding what *ought* to be done. This form of reasoning is, for Aristotle, 'generically different' from technical reasoning and involves proceeding in a measured or 'deliberative fashion'.[23]

Although, in deliberative reasoning, both the means and ends of action are open to question, what is deliberated upon is not ends but means. However, it would be quite wrong to infer from this that means and ends can be characterized independently of each other. In choosing between alternative means, practitioners must also reflect on the alternative ethical ends which supply them with criteria for their choice. If the alternative means are simply different ways of achieving the same ethical end, then the question is simply an instrumental question about their relative effectiveness. Where, however, alternative means are means to different ethical ends, then the practitioner has to deliberate about these ends as possible alternative means to some further all-embracing end. Thus, deliberation is not a way of resolving technical problems for which there is, in principle, some correct answer. Rather, it is a way of resolving those moral dilemmas which occur when different ethically desirable ends entail different, and perhaps incompatible, courses of action.

The formal structure of deliberative reasoning is that of the practical syllogism, where the major premise is a practical principle stating what in general ought to be done (e.g. people with personal difficulties ought to be treated with consideration) and the minor premise asserts a particular instance falling under this major premise (this person has just lost his wife). Thus, the method of deliberative reasoning is, like the hypothetico-deductive method of scientific reasoning, effected through a syllogistic argument in which a particular case is subsumed under a general principle. But the practical syllogism differs from the ordinary syllogism in at least two crucial respects.

First, the conclusion of a practical syllogism is not a statement prescribing 'what ought to be done' which is analogous to the statements describing 'what is the case' with which ordinary syllogisms conclude. The conclusion of a practical syllogism is an *action* which, precisely because it issues from a deliberate process of moving from premises to conclusions, is the outcome of a process of reasoning rather than shrewd guess-work or pure chance. Second, this action, though the product of deductively valid reasoning, is not 'right' action in the sense that it has been proved to be correct. It is 'right' action because it is *reasoned* action that can be defended discursively in argument and justified as morally appropriate to the particular circumstances in which it was taken.[24] Moreover, in deliberative reasoning, it is always conceded that there may be more than one ethical principle that can supply the content to a major premise and that there is no formula for methodically determining which one should be invoked in a particular practical situation. It is for this reason that Aristotle insists that collective deliberation by the many is always preferable to the isolated deliberation of the individual.

It is for this reason, too, that good deliberation is entirely dependent on the possession of what Aristotle calls *phronesis*, which we would translate as 'practical wisdom'. *Phronesis* is the virtue of knowing which general ethical principle to apply in a particular situation. For Aristotle, *phronesis* is the supreme intellectual virtue and an indispensable feature of practice. The *phronimos* – the man of practical wisdom – is the man who sees the particularities of his practical situation in the light of their ethical significance and acts consistently on this basis. Without practical wisdom, deliberation degenerates into an intellectual exercise, and 'good practice' becomes indistinguishable from instrumental cleverness. The man who lacks *phronesis* may be technically accountable, but he can never be morally answerable.

Hence, 'practical wisdom' is manifest in a knowledge of what is required in a particular moral situation, and a willingness to act so that this knowledge can take a concrete form. It is a comprehensive moral capacity which combines practical knowledge of the good with sound judgement about what, in a particular situation, would constitute an appropriate expression of this good. For this reason 'judgement' is an essential element in practical wisdom. But it is not the judgement of the umpire impartially applying a set of codified rules. Rather, it is that form of wise and prudent judgement which takes account of what would be morally appropriate and fitting in a particular situation.[25]

'Judgement' is thus a crucial term in the equation linking deliberation and practical wisdom with action. Deliberating well is a mark of *phronesis*, and *phronesis* is the union of good judgement and action. What is distinctive of the *phronimos* is that her or his deliberations lead, by way of judgement, to practice. And what is distinctive of practice is that it bears a constitutive relationship to practical knowledge, deliberation and the pursuit of the human good. It is this concept of practice from which our own concept has evolved and, if my argument is correct, it is this concept of practice which will better enable us to answer the question posed in the title of this chapter. It is to this question that I now wish to return.

V

One of my main aims has been to show how a self-conscious awareness of the historical roots of the concept of practice helps us to understand why current attempts to analyse the concepts run into the sort of difficulties that they do. Another has been to show how these difficulties are largely the product of the widespread assumption that practice can only be adequately analysed by means of an ahistorical inquiry into the kind of relationship to theory that it may, or may not, have. Because of this, the conceptual distinctions crucial for any philosophical elucidation of what constitutes an educational practice are always drawn at the wrong point. For what the history of the concept reveals is that the important conceptual distinctions are not those between theory and practice, knowledge and action, or 'knowing-how' and 'knowing-that'. Rather, they are distinctions between different kinds of action (*poiesis* and *praxis*, ethically enlightened action and technical effective action) and the forms of knowledge appropriate to them (*techne* and *phronesis*, technical knowledge and practical knowledge). What, in effect, I have tried to show is that the failure to recognize the importance of these distinctions has left our concept of practice confused. As a result, our understanding of why education is construed as a practice has become increasingly difficult to articulate and describe.

Once the importance of these distinctions is acknowledged, it becomes clear why characterizations of educational practice which focus on its relationship to theory always break down. It becomes clear, for example, that since educational practice is always guided by some theory about the ethical goods internal to that practice, it cannot be made intelligible in terms of an opposition to theory. But at the same time, it becomes equally clear why this does not mean that educational practice can be sufficiently characterized as a theory-guided pursuit. For what is distinctive of an educational practice is that it is guided not just by some general practical theory, but also by the exigencies of the practical situation in which this theory is to be applied. Thus, the guidance given by theory always has to be moderated by the guidance given by *phronesis* – wise and prudent judgement about if, and to what extent, this 'theory' ought to be invoked and enacted in a concrete case.

The fact that educational practice cannot be properly characterized as 'theory-dependent' or 'theory-guided' should not be taken to add credibility to the view that it is simply a species of theory-free 'know-how' of a Rylean kind. What is distinctive of *praxis* is that it is a form of reflexive action which can itself transform the 'theory' which guides it. *Poiesis* is a form of non-reflexive 'know-how' precisely because it does not itself change its guiding *techne*. For praxis, however, theory is as subject to change as is practice itself. Neither theory nor practice is pre-eminent: each is continuously being modified and revised by the other.

Educational practice cannot be made intelligible as a form of *poiesis* guided by fixed ends and governed by determinate rules. It can only be made intelligible as a form of *praxis* guided by ethical criteria immanent in educational practice itself: criteria which serve to distinguish genuine educational practices from those that are not, and good educational practice from that which is indifferent or bad. While some people now want to reduce educational practice to a kind of 'making action' through which some raw material can be moulded into a pre-specifiable shape, educational practitioners continue to experience it as a species of 'doing action' governed by complex and sometimes competing ethical ends which may themselves be modified in the light of practical circumstances and particular conditions. It is in these terms that many educational practitioners understand their work. And it is in terms provided by the concepts and language of *praxis* that many of them would want to define and defend the essential features of their educational and professional role.

'What is an educational practice?' The answer I have tried to provide is one which is firmly grounded in those developments in post-analytic philosophy which seek to re-establish the classic concept of *praxis* in the modern world.[26] Clearly, any further elaboration of this answer would benefit from a close inspection of the attempts in curriculum theory, evaluation and research to create a renewed awareness of educational practice as the achievement of a tradition rather than as a form of craft-knowledge or technical expertise.[27] What is also clear is that one of the implications of this answer is that it anticipates a discussion about the future of the philosophy of education which starts from a view about 'what a practice is' rather than a view about 'what philosophy is'. It thus foreshadows the re-emergence of educational philosophy as a species of 'practical philosophy' explicitly, committed to that concept of practice which has always provided education with its primary definition. Within our dominant contemporary culture, this concept of practice has been rendered marginal and now faces something approaching total effacement. As new concepts of educational practice are emerging, so the older concepts of practical wisdom, deliberation and judgement are being eroded. It is thus only by reaffirming its traditional role that the philosophy of education will be better able to promote the integrity of educational practice and oppose all those cultural tendencies which now undermine and degrade it.

PART II: TOWARDS A CRITICAL EDUCATIONAL SCIENCE

5 CAN EDUCATIONAL RESEARCH BE SCIENTIFIC?

> An educational science is any portion of ascertained
> knowledge that would enter into the heart, head and hands
> of educators and which, by entering in render the
> performance of the educational function more enlightened.[1]

I

Philosophical interest in the idea of an educational science is hardly new. During the second half of the nineteenth century, Spencer, Huxley, Bain and others argued that many of the intransigent problems of education could only be solved by enlisting the experimental methods of the natural sciences. Subsequent experience has done little to support this early optimism and it comes as no surprise to find that recent opinion about the role of science in education is deeply divided. This division has many facets and takes many forms. Within the philosophy of education it emerged as a dispute about whether the concept of 'educational theory' should be constrained by purely scientific canons of rationality or whether it should be more generously interpreted so as to incorporate various others 'forms of knowledge'.[2] Within the educational research community, however, the point at issue has not been the degree to which educational theories should be subject to scientific standards but the more basic question of whether scientific standards have any place in educational research at all. Here the arguments have centred on whether educational research should follow recent intellectual trends and employ the kind of non-scientific methodologies that now hold sway in the social sciences. The first significant steps in this 'new direction' were, of course, made by the phenomenologically inspired sociology of education[3] and they were clearly evident in the efforts to make educational research 'illuminative' and 'qualitative' rather than 'statistical' and 'quantitative'.[4]

Although the educational researchers engaged in these methodological arguments did not appeal to philosophical considerations, they have nevertheless supported their respective positions by tacitly invoking one or other of the two dominant philosophical attitudes towards the nature of the social sciences.[5] Hence, while naturalism, the doctrine that the social sciences should replicate the aims and methods of the natural sciences, is frequently espoused in the opening chapters of most textbooks on educational research,[6] the alternative interpretive view, which holds that because social action is intentional and rule-governed it cannot be studied 'scientifically', is invoked to provide a philosophical rationale for all those methodological positions which posit a sharp cleavage between the natural and the social sciences.[7] In contrast to naturalism, therefore, interpretive approaches to educational research insist that their principal task is not to construct scientific theories that can be experimentally tested, but to construct interpretive accounts which grasp the intelligibility and coherence of social action by revealing the meaning it has to those who perform it.[8]

The difference between these two conceptions of educational research are, of course, but a particular reflection of the general controversy that has dominated the entire history of the philosophy of the social sciences.[9] However, what, for present purposes, is of interest is how the very process of importing this controversy into discussions about the nature of educational research has led to the neglect of some important philosophical issues. For example, simply by giving credence to the belief that the philosophical basis of educational research can be understood in terms of the traditional discourse of the philosophy of the social sciences, the logically prior question of determining whether educational research is indeed a social science is left untouched. Similarly, a preoccupation with a controversy in which it is assumed that scientific explanation and interpretive understanding are mutually exclusive goals neglects the task of exploring the effects of this assumption on the scientific aspirations of a research activity directed towards a practical field like education. In short, the conventional assumption that aims and structures for educational research can be derived from one or other of the two dominant traditions of social scientific inquiry conceals how it is only by first examining the way in which the *educational* character of research is to be understood that the question of its scientific status can be appraised. It is with these distinctly educational issues that this chapter is concerned.

II

In educational research textbooks, the question 'what is educational research?' is invariably construed as a request for a description of the various aims, methods and procedures employed by educational researchers. However, as well as this descriptive interpretation, the question may also be construed as a request for the evaluative criteria in terms of which the adequacy any of these various aims, methods and procedures can be judged. Clearly, if there are no real differences between research which is 'educational' and research which is not, there are no real grounds for using this term to designate one form of research rather than any other. Alternatively, if there are such differences, these cannot be distilled from a descriptive survey of the current activities of educational researchers. Answering a question like 'what is educational research?' by reading off standards from the actual practices of those claiming to be engaged in this activity merely prejudges the question in a way favourable to those making this claim and so begs the very question at issue. For this reason, questions about the nature of educational research are not questions about the numerous ways in which this enterprise is conventionally interpreted, so much as requests to spell out those distinctive features of this activity in terms of which the adequacy of each and any of these conventional interpretations can be appraised.

What, then, are the distinctive features of educational research? An initial step towards answering this question involves making two familiar points about the structure of human activities.[10] These are, first, that human activities can only be adequately characterized by reference to the overall purpose for which they are undertaken. Hence, a particular research activity is only made intelligible as an activity of that kind by reference to its particular purpose, and a particular research practice can only be understood as a practice of this activity by seeing it as contributing to this purpose. Second, the general purpose characterizing any human activity is either theoretical or practical depending on whether it aims to discover something or to bring about change. Clearly most research activities are theoretical in the sense that their distinctive purpose is to resolve theoretical problems by discovering new knowledge. Determining the distinguishing purpose of educational research, however, is complicated by the fact that education is not itself a theoretical activity, but a practical activity the purpose of which is to change those being educated in some desirable ways. This implies that educational research cannot be defined simply by reference to the sort of purposes appropriate to research activities concerned to resolve theoretical problems but must instead operate within the framework of practical ends in terms of which educational activities are conducted. Hence, while educational research is, like any other research activity, concerned to investigate and resolve problems, it differs from theoretical research in the sense that the educational problems it seeks to address are always practical problems, which, as such, cannot be resolved by the discovery of new knowledge. As Gauthier says: 'practical problems are problems about what to do . . . their solution is only found in doing something'.[11]

At the outset, then, it is important to recognize that since it is the investigation of educational problems that provides educational research with whatever distinctive purpose it may have, the testing ground for educational research is not its ability to conform to criteria derived from the social sciences, but its capacity to confront these problems in a systematic way. For this reason, any account of the nature of educational research that simply transforms educational problems into a series of theoretical problems seriously distorts the purpose of the whole enterprise. Indeed, to disregard the practical nature of educational problems in this way so deprives them of whatever educational character they may have, as to ensure that any claim to be engaged in *educational* research, rather than some form of social scientific research, cannot be seriously maintained.

How do problems occur? Generally, theoretical problems occur when what is believed to be the case is not the case. They arise, in other words, when events occur which are inexplicable in terms of existing beliefs and knowledge, and the purpose of theoretical research is to overcome these discrepancies by producing new theories which ensure that what was previously problematic will no longer be so. In this sense, theoretical problems provide the fundamental link between theories and the world; for it is only by resolving these problems that the degree of accuracy with which theories depict the world is improved.[12]

It follows from this that theoretical problems do not arise out of a theoretical vacuum but, instead, always reflect and result from the theoretical background against which they occur. The problems of social scientific research, therefore, are not determined by inadequacies in any of the social practices or human activities which such research may seek to explain, but by inadequacies in the theoretical framework in terms of which these investigations are conducted. For example, psychological problems about learning are not determined by the practical problems experienced by learners but by the psychological theory of learning that guides those engaged in this kind of research.

Educational problems, being practical problems, are not governed by the rules and norms of theoretical research. Rather, they occur when the practices employed in educational activities are in some sense inadequate to their purpose. They arise, in other words, when there is some discrepancy between an educational practice and the expectations with which this practice is undertaken. The fact that educational problems occur because of this kind of non-fulfilment of expectations is informative, for to have expectations of a practice necessarily implies the possession of some prior beliefs by virtue of which these expectations are explained and justified.[13] Since, in this sense, those engaged in educational activities are already committed to some elaborate, if not explicit, set of beliefs about what they are doing, they, no less than those engaged in theoretical research, must also possess some theoretical framework that serves to explain and direct their practices. An educational problem, therefore, in denoting the failure of a practice, also denotes a failure in the theory from which a belief in the efficacy of this practice is derived. By undermining the expectations of an educational practice, an educational problem undermines the validity of some logically prior educational theory.

Given this account of educational problems, the concepts of educational theory and practice acquire meanings rather different from those normally employed in educational research. Thus, if educational problems are theory-dependent then all educational practice is theory-laden too. The very identification of an educational practice always depends on grasping the framework of thought that makes it count as a practice of that sort. Second, if educational practice is always embedded in theory, then there is nothing to which the notion of 'educational theory' can coherently refer, other than the theory that guides the practice of those engaged in educational pursuits. An educational theory, therefore, is not something 'derived from' or 'based on' the theories *about* education that are produced by the theoretical social sciences. Nor is it something that can be mechanically attached to practice in the form of problem-solving guidance. Rather, like sociological or psychological theory, it refers to a conceptual framework that expresses how those engaged in some particular activity ought to proceed.

If theory and practice are understood in this way it follows that the 'gap' between them refers to the *source* of the educational problems to which educational theorizing should be addressed. All problems are reflections of a gap between theory and practice. Just as theoretical problems reflect a gap between a theory and the reality that this theory purports to describe, so an educational problem reveals a failure to reconcile the realities of practice with the theoretical framework within which these practices are experienced and understood. Closing the gap between theory and practice, therefore, is not a matter of finding ways of improving the practical effectiveness of social scientific theories but one of improving the theories employed by practitioners to make sense of their practices. So interpreted, reducing the gap between theory and practice is the *raison d'être* of educational theorizing, rather than something that has to be done *after* the theory has been completed but *before* it can be effectively applied.

Once the relationship between educational theory, practice and problems is understood in this way, the strengths and weaknesses of naturalist and interpretive approaches can be more readily assessed. One of the obvious strengths of the naturalist approach is its aspiration to adopt methodological principles designed to guard against the intrusion of subjectivity, prejudice and bias. Another is its claim that there may be factors operative in educational situations which remain opaque to the self-understandings of practitioners and cannot be explained by reference to their intentions and beliefs. However, although naturalist approaches to educational research properly refuse to be confined to the concepts and beliefs of educational practitioners, they mistakenly infer from this that solutions to educational problems can be produced without any reference to the framework of thought in terms of which these problems arise. This failure to consider the relationship between natural scientific concepts and theories on the one hand, and the concepts and theories informing educational practice on the other, means that the theoretical powers of educational practitioners are overlooked and so ensures a failure to appreciate how educational problems are generated out of the experiences of practitioners and only emerge when the ways in which these experiences are usually organized are found to be inadequate. Because it is not directly concerned to help practitioners organize their experiences more adequately, the naturalist view of educational research is not really concerned with *educational* problems at all.

The major strengths of the interpretive approach derive from its firm insistence that educational research must be rooted in the concepts and theories of educational practitioners. However, the crucial weakness of the approach is that from the correct observation that educational research must be interpretive, it infers that this exhausts the purpose of the enterprise. But to concede that educational problems arise out of the ideas and beliefs of educational practitioners is not to accept that these ideas and beliefs are true. Practitioners' beliefs and preconceptions, although they may be constitutive of their practices, are also beliefs and preconceptions about the nature of the situation in which they are operating and about the sort of consequences that their practices will have. As such they always entail some minimal claims about the way things are, which may turn out to be erroneous or false. Moreover, unless some distinction can be made between what practitioners think or believe they are doing and what they are doing, unless, that is, concrete realities impinge upon educational practices in a way not wholly determined by the practitioner's frame of mind, there would not be any educational problems as such. It is precisely because there is some difference between what actually happens when practitioners engage in educational pursuits and their more or less accurate understanding of what is happening, that educational problems occur.

Any research concerned to resolve educational problems, therefore, cannot rest content with explicating practitioners' own interpretations, but must also be prepared critically to evaluate them and to suggest alternative explanations that are in some sense better. This kind of research will not be limited to producing descriptive records of practitioners' own understandings. On the contrary, by recognizing that educational problems arise precisely because such understandings are incoherent, by seeking to reveal how they are a consequence of these incoherences, and by investigating them in terms opposed to those of practitioners, such research will be critical of practitioners' interpretations and seek to create alternative theories that are incompatible with them. The interpretive approach, by restricting its goal to one of explicating the ways in which educational practices are made intelligible, neglects the importance of all those cases in which practitioners' experiences and self-understandings are at variance with their actual situation, and so ignores precisely those elements of educational experience that are of most importance to educational research. In effect, by failing to identify and recognize practitioners' misunderstandings, the interpretive approach deprives itself of any means of confronting the problems these misunderstandings create. For this reason, it excludes any real concern with educational *problems* at all.

Looked at in this way, it is evident that naturalist and interpretive approaches to educational research are such that the strengths of one are the weaknesses of the other. The naturalist approach, by adopting methodologies designed to assess and improve the rationality of scientific theories and beliefs, offers no way of assessing and improving the rationality of the educational theories and beliefs that govern educational practice. In consequence, it fails to appreciate the crucial role that rationality plays in educational practice and that its assessment plays in educational research. Indeed, by refusing to regard practice as a source of theory in its own right, the naturalist approach effectively eliminates the educational character of the problems it purports to confront. The interpretive approach, though concerned to expose the structure of rationality informing educational practice, refuses to recognize any evaluative criteria in terms of which this rationality can be appraised. And by so insulating the self-understandings of practitioners from direct criticism, the interpretive approach effectively eliminates the problematic character of the practices it seeks to portray.

III

The lesson to be drawn from the foregoing analysis is not that naturalist and interpretive accounts of educational research are false but that each offers only a partial, one-sided realization of what any adequate philosophical account of the nature of educational research requires. What needs to be recognized, therefore, is that any attempt to reduce educational research to *either* a natural *or* an interpretive science overlooks the twin features central to any distinctively educational science. First, it is an *educational* science, which is to say that it investigates a consciously performed practical activity which can only be identified and understood by reference to the meaning it has for those who practice it. Second, it is an educational *science*, which is to say that it tries to develop theories that explain and resolve the problems to which the practice of this activity gives rise. What is required, therefore, is a view of educational research which is 'interpretive' in the sense that its theories are grounded in the perspectives of educational practice and 'scientific' in the sense that these theories provide a coherent challenge to the interpretations which practitioners actually employ.

If educational research is both interpretive and scientific how are these twin features to be reconciled? More particularly, how does the pre-interpreted nature of educational problems affect their scientific solution? The widespread belief that the scientific status of educational research can only be secured if the practical and interpretive features of educational problems are disregarded is primarily owing to the fact that the version of naturalism enjoying a position of near orthodoxy in educational research is one which relies on the hypothetico-deductive account of science suggested by logical empiricism. With this version of naturalism, neither the practical nature of educational problems nor the interpretive framework within which they occur has any bearing on the question of their scientific solution. On this view, science is not concerned with how problems arise. Nor are the motives, intentions or practical purposes of those for whom they occur of any great importance. All that matters is that these problems can be reformulated in a way that allows hypothetical solutions to be proposed which can then be tested by assessing their deductive implications against observed results. The insistence that the hallmark of scientific theories is their deductive validity and empirical testability is vital, for it is precisely their amenability to these requirements that ensures that they are scientific rather than ideological or metaphysical.

The reason why this view of science is so appealing to educational research is obvious enough. Close conformity to hypothetico-deductive methods would demonstrate that educational research was a 'value-free' activity concerned only with the rational evaluation of hypotheses. Moreover, if the findings of scientific research were brought to bear on educational problems, objective solutions could be found which were based on neutral evidence rather than subjective opinion. It is therefore only by embracing the impersonal and impartial logic of hypothetico-deductive reasoning that subjective bias can be expunged from educational research and the goal of creating a scientifically validated body of 'value-free' educational theory can be pursued in an atmosphere undisturbed by the clash of rival interpretations and subjective prejudices.

Despite these obvious attractions, the hypothetico-deductive account has always been vulnerable to numerous objections which the philosophy of science has, throughout its history, made many unsuccessful efforts to counteract.[14] In recent times, the reason why these problems persist has become clearly apparent. Put briefly, it is because they are firmly embedded in the empiricist philosophical foundations on which the hypothetico-deductive image of science has been erected, and arise out of the deep-seated presumption that logic is the primary tool for assessing the scientific status of theories. As a result of these insights, confidence in the capacity of logical empiricism to provide an adequate epistemological basis for science has been severely eroded and has given way to a 'post-empiricist' philosophy of science that does not rely on an analysis of the logical status of scientific theories, but on detailed historical studies of the process of scientific progress and change.[15]

Despite the many differences among those initially responsible for developing this new philosophy of science, they share sufficient common ground for an image of science to emerge which is very different from the orthodox view. What, more than anything, provides this common ground is a uniform agreement both about the impossibility of a theory-free observational language and about the implications of this for an understanding of science. Rapidly stated, these implications are, first, that since the relation between observed results and the scientific status of theories is not as simple as traditionally assumed, science cannot be a process of testing theories in accordance with impersonal observation. Indeed, far from being the result of scientific inquiry, theory actively guides its conduct. Second, if observation can neither confirm nor refute scientific theories, all scientific knowledge has a permanently provisional character. 'Truth' may provide a regulative ideal in the construction of theories but it has no relevance to their evaluation. Finally, the fallibility of all scientific theories means that scientific progress cannot be a cumulative process in which a corpus of true knowledge is painstakingly collected. Rather, science develops because of the 'problem situations' that accompany its commitment to some prior theoretical framework. It is by pursuing the 'research programme' that this framework suggests and by confronting the problems that its 'positive heuristic' provides that science is able to progress in an orderly and systematic fashion.[16] These problems, by stimulating a need to develop new theories out of the failure of their predecessors, ensure progressive theoretical innovation and guarantee the continuity of research.

The realization that it is continuing research rather than accumulated results that provides the life-blood of science makes it clear that the core of science is not the rational justification applicable to its theoretical end-products but the rational features of the processes of scientific discovery, innovation and change. Scientific rationality is not simply a matter of conforming to a set of unambiguous methodological rules. Nor is it to be identified with the exclusion of fallible human judgement. Rather it is identified with the criteria of 'rational acceptability'[17] according to which practical judgements about which theories to accept and which to reject are made and justified. Accepting a theory because it solves or eliminates problems, or provides a guide to further research, rejecting another because it fails to solve its own problems, or is irrelevant to the problem in hand, involves human judgements that are rational rather than arbitrary because, given the context, there are grounds on which they can be justified and defended. The fact that such judgements are made without the benefit of infallible reasoning procedures that guarantee their truth or make them immune from further criticism does not mean that they are irrational. Nor does it mean that the results of logic and evidence are irrelevant. What it means is that these results have to be interpreted in the light of the particular context to which they relate, and evaluated in the light of the particular problem-situation under consideration. And it is the norms and principles governing this process of interpretation and evaluation that provide the paradigm of scientific rationality.[18]

Although the precise articulation of these norms and principles remains an outstanding task, there is little doubt that a historically based philosophy of science constitutes a significant improvement over traditional empiricism and suggests a more sophisticated understanding both of the nature of science and of its relationship to education. In particular, by exposing how scientific inquiry proceeds only by reference to some prior interpretive framework, it reveals not only how science and education are both theory-guided activities but also how their respective guiding theories share some common features. For example, it reveals how both are the product of on-going historical traditions and, as such, constitute the modes of thought appropriate to the social context in which the respective activities are undertaken. In effect, science and education operate in distinctive social communities whose practices are governed by beliefs, attitudes and expectations that are inherited and prescribed. Just because the guiding theory of a particular science may involve a self-conscious immersion in 'methodology' does not alter the fact that it is, like the guiding theory of educational practice, a way of thinking that is transmitted through tradition and acquired through a process of initiation.

Science and education are also similar in that their practitioners resolve problems by formulating judgements in the light of the theoretical frameworks they already possess. Although these theoretical preconceptions are, in both cases, the product of precedent and tradition, what is distinctive about the problem-solving judgements of science is that they are governed by norms and principles designed to expose and eliminate the inadequacies in existing theoretical understanding and hence to encourage progressive, theoretical development and change. What is distinctive about educational judgements, however, is that the truth of the beliefs and theories by which they are informed is accepted in a largely uncritical and non-reflective way. It is this unquestioning 'common-sense' attitude that makes conventional educational thinking unscientific by making the problems it creates immune from scientific analysis and resolution.[19]

If science and education are understood in this way it becomes apparent that the naturalist demand for educational research to become scientific does not entail that practical educational problems must be assimilated to theoretical social scientific problems. Not does it mean that educational research must be conducted in close conformity with some purely formal account of 'the scientific method'. Rather, it is a demand for educational research to develop methodological principles and procedures that will emancipate practitioners from their dependence on habit and traditions so that their interpretations and judgements become more closely governed by those standards of rationality that are conducive to scientific progress and on which the well-being of any science depends. This does not imply that practical educational thinking must be abandoned in favour of the conceptual schemes of the social sciences. Nor does it involve distorting practical educational experience by the imposition of theories which have been developed for social scientific areas of inquiry and which always predetermine what the relevant research problems and categories are going to be. What is being abandoned is an unscientific attitude towards established educational interpretations so that the beliefs and justifications through which they are sustained can be systematically challenged and changed. It is not by the replacement of existing educational theories but through their improvement that the judgements of practitioners will be enriched by scientific virtues and thereby acquire a more rational character.

Clearly, for educational research to become scientific in this sense, some modifications to existing research procedures would be necessary. For example, the idea that theory can be scientifically tested independently of practice and then used to correct or assess any educational practice would have to be replaced by the diametrically opposite view that an educational theory only acquires a scientific character if it can itself be corrected and assessed in the light of its practical consequences. Second, the fact that it is the interpretations of educational practitioners that provide both the subject matter for educational research and the testing ground for its results would make it entirely inappropriate to regard teachers as objects for theoretical inspection, as consumers who apply solutions or as clients to whom researchers address their findings and reports. Rather, since the problems that educational research seeks to confront only arise for educational practitioners, it would be recognized that their active participation in the research enterprise is an indispensable necessity. Indeed, it is only with the successful repudiation of all those divisions and distinctions that at present separate the research community from the educational community that the possibility of research which is both educational and scientific can be secured.

6 PHILOSOPHY, VALUES AND EDUCATIONAL SCIENCE

> Can those who carry out educational research safely ignore
> that part of their subject (philosophy) which underlies their
> own investigations? For if we do so we cannot claim to be
> educationalists but must be content with being . . .
> laboratory technicians . . . If we are merely technicians, we
> cannot claim to be able to criticize the educational
> foundations and implications of our own work. This means
> quite simply that we cannot claim to know what we are
> doing.[1]

I

There is a long and honourable tradition of educational research which is not
so much concerned with producing theoretical knowledge about education as
with providing practical knowledge for guiding the conduct of educational
pursuits. This tradition derives much of its inspiration from Aristotle. It was he
who initiated the search for the form of rationality appropriate to practical
thought and action; and it is he who remains the chief spokesman for a view of
educational research as a form of 'practical philosophy' in which answers to
questions about educational aims and goals are sought in metaphysical theories of human nature and moral beliefs about the good for man.

Today, of course, this tradition has virtually disappeared. Educational
philosophy is no longer concerned with metaphysical and moral themes and
educational research is now governed by a style of thought in which any

commitment to educational values is treated with suspicion and mistrust. Indeed, the distance separating modern and traditional attitudes to the study of education has become so astronomic that educational researchers are now able to characterize their activity by contrasting it to the traditional educational philosophy it has replaced. Educational philosophy, they point out, was a prescriptive enterprise motivated by subjective preference and ideological intent; its theories were based on little more than *a priori* metaphysical speculation and value-laden dogma. Educational research, however, is neither metaphysical nor prescriptive; it is an empirical and value-free enterprise motivated only by a disinterested search for knowledge and understanding. Indeed, many educational researchers would maintain that it is only because they now adopt methods specifically designed to liberate research from 'practical philosophy' that they can justify their claim to be creating a body of educational theory that is uncontaminated by personal educational values or rival metaphysical beliefs.[2]

What I am going to suggest is that metaphysical and moral beliefs cannot be expelled from educational research in this way and that educational research requires much more in the way of a relationship to 'practical philosophy' than most educational researchers are prepared to recognize or admit. The reason why this is so is that educational research, though it may have the appearance of a disinterested and impersonal pursuit, always involves a commitment to some educational philosophy and hence to the educational values that such a commitment unavoidably entails. Thus, although educational researchers may, and usually do, study education without articulating any philosophical beliefs or educational values, this should not be taken to indicate that philosophy and values do not permeate their work. All that it indicates is the success of educational research in concealing the moral and philosophical commitments to which it always implicitly subscribes.

So much for my general position. In what follows I intend to develop and defend this position by developing and defending the following specific claims.

1 Values are so vital an ingredient in educational research that their elimination is impossible save by eliminating the research enterprise itself. Those educational researchers who claim that they are adopting a 'disinterested' stance are, therefore, simply failing to recognize certain features of their work.

2 The reason why educational research is always value-laden is because educational research methods always entail a commitment to some educational philosophy. 'Educational research' and 'educational philosophy' are not, therefore, as independent as is usually thought and any separation of the two represents a historically contingent division of labour rather than any clear cut differences in purpose.

3 To accept that philosophy and values cannot be expunged from educational research is not to concede that educational research cannot be a scientific pursuit. On the contrary, any coherent account of an educational science requires that the relationship between philosophy, values and educational

research be formulated in a way that renders them compatible rather than antithetical.

The purpose of the remainder of this chapter is to restate these three claims in more concrete detail.

II

Educational researchers have always recognized that values may intrude into the conduct of their work. They have, for example, always conceded that values influence their choice of research problems and their views about the practical uses their research results should serve. However, these same educational researchers have always assumed that by making certain standard moves, any problems posed by this threat of value-infiltration can easily be neutralized. For example, by separating the 'context of discovery' from 'the context of justification', educational researchers believe they can divorce the objective logic in terms of which theories are validated from the subjective values which determined their choice. As a result, the values that initially prompt the selection of research problems can be safely ignored on the grounds that they relate to the pre-scientific aspects of research inquiry. Likewise, by separating the 'value-free' methods of theory testing from 'value-laden' questions concerning their practical use, most educational researchers believe that educational research can be insulated from any suspicion of having a special interest in its own case.[3]

Over the past two decades, these familiar strategies for eliminating the problem of value-intrusion have begun to crumble under the impact of a prolonged onslaught emanating from sources as varied as the philosophy of language,[4] neo-Marxist social theory,[5] political theory[6] and the philosophy of science.[7] The initial shots in this attack were, of course, fired by Thomas Kuhn's image of the natural scientist as a member of an ideological community which demanded, as the price of membership, an allegiance to the value-commitments of the dominant 'paradigm'.[8] More illuminating for present purposes, however, is a whole series of methodological studies in political philosophy which reveal how certain political values tend to support certain forms of social science and, conversely, how certain forms of social science sustain certain political values.[9] One of the earliest attempts to articulate this line of thought was Charles Taylor's argument that 'the adoption of a framework of explanation carries with it the adoption of the "value-slope" implicit in it'.[10] Summarily stated, Taylor's argument runs as follows. Since political phenomena may be classified in an indefinite number of ways, political researchers must devise theoretical frameworks for classifying and interpreting political phenomena in ways relevant to the elaboration of adequate explanations. However, Taylor argues, it is just this kind of theoretical framework that political philosophers have traditionally devised in order to evaluate or advocate particular political values. Clearly, therefore, the explanatory frameworks used by political researchers to identify and explain the relevant features of political phenomena can be either compatible or incompatible with the theoretical framework operative in different political philosophies. Where they are compatible, the explanations of political research and the prescriptive conclusions of political philosophy will tend to be mutually reinforcing. Where they are not, then either the research results will make the political philosophy appear untenable or the political philosophy will interpret the research results as irrelevant or misconceived.

The conclusion Taylor draws from this is not just the familiar point that a political researcher's choice of explanatory framework determines the areas she studies or the questions she asks. Rather it is that with certain explanatory frameworks some political values will be reinforced and others undermined. Taylor summarizes his views in the following way:

> We can say that a given explanatory framework secretes a notion of good, and a set of valuations which cannot be done away with – though they can be over-ridden – unless we do away with the framework . . . this is enough to show that the neutrality of the findings of political science is not what it was thought to be. For establishing a given framework restricts the range of value positions which can be defensively adopted . . . The framework can be said to describe the onus of argument in a certain way. It is thus not neutral.[11]

Since its initial appearance, Taylor's position has received detailed and extensive support and the range of critical literature showing the value-ladenness of the social sciences is now extensive.[12] Despite its widespread acceptance, however, the implications of Taylor's view for educational research are rarely conceded. For example, it is rarely conceded that if, as Taylor claims, the adoption of a theoretical standpoint in political research always involves the adoption of a political standpoint, then the conventional view that educational research does not incorporate an educational standpoint becomes, to say the least, suspect. The phenomena of education, no less than the phenomena of politics, are always much more than a source of empirical constraint on the explanatory theories of educational researchers, and educational research is always much more related to values than is generally recognized. Similarly, although Taylor's arguments make it clear that the logical connection between political values and social science is because of the formal similarities between the theoretical frameworks of the social sciences and the theoretical frameworks of political philosophy, the implications of this for an understanding of the relationship between educational research and educational philosophy have remained virtually unexplored. This provides a useful point of entry to my second claim, which is that any particular research methodology always incorporates a particular educational philosophy.

III

For a long time now, it has been agreed that what distinguishes the prescriptive theories of traditional educational philosophy from the empirical theories of educational research is that the former contain metaphysical elements which the latter do not. Indeed, one of the long-standing orthodoxies of the philosophy of education is the view that the educational philosophies of Plato, Rousseau, Dewey and the rest all try to show how certain global educational aims can be supported by general metaphysical assumptions about human nature.[13] In a familiar version of this argument, T. W. Moore defined these traditional educational philosophies as 'general theories of education' which, since they prescribe the 'production of a particular type of person', necessarily presuppose 'assumptions about human nature'.[14] However, because these assumptions are metaphysical assumptions, they have always been the cause of some philosophical unease.

In the past, assumptions of a substantial nature about children were often derived, supposedly, from metaphysical views of the nature of man . . . A general criticism of assumptions like these is that they are of the wrong kind for a theory of education . . . they are *a priori* assumptions adopted ahead of experience and often of the kind that experience can do nothing to refute.[15]

Moore's response to this deficiency was to offer the standard philosophical recommendation:

What is needed in an educational theory is an accurate factual picture of human nature . . . and this can only come from . . . scientific studies of children themselves. Piaget, Freud, Kohlberg and others . . . have more to offer in this respect than the great names in traditional educational theory.[16]

What is worth noticing is how all those who share this view tend to overlook three important and largely uncontroversial developments in the philosophy of the social sciences. In the first place, by arguing for educational theories in which metaphysical views of human nature are replaced by 'an accurate factual picture', they ignore the extent to which non-educational philosophers are now agreed that metaphysical views of human nature are indispensable to the empirical social sciences. Numerous studies could be cited,[17] but for present purposes the following example makes the general point clearly enough:

The old insistence on an essential human nature gave rise to social theories which were metaphysical and normative. Orthodox modern theories, by contrast, strive to be empirical and ethically neutral. Given the textbook canons of empirical science, models of man become metaphysical posits without utility or justification . . . Empiricism has triumphed and traditional assumptions are dead and buried . . . They are buried perhaps, but certainly not dead. They are buried in the roots of the very theories which purport to explain them. There is no dispensing with a model of man . . . Every social theory needs a metaphysic . . . in which a model of man and a method of science complement each other.[18]

Since metaphysical theories of human nature are as indispensable to the social sciences as they are to 'general theories of education', those educational philosophers who look to social scientific inquiries for an 'empirical' theory of human nature will simply reaffirm whatever metaphysical theory these inquiries presuppose and hence always beg the very question at issue.[19] It is no doubt because of this oversight that they also fail to notice that, just as different metaphysical theories of human nature account for the emergence of a variety of educational philosophies, so it is precisely the same kind of differences that account for the emergence of a variety of approaches to the social sciences.[20] The obvious example is provided by the way in which different models of human nature have spawned quite different models of psychology:

> How human nature is to be conceptualised is clearly the most important . . . decision which a psychological theory must make . . . Some of the choices which a psychology faces in constituting its core concept of human nature . . . include: taking behaviour or consciousness to be the more fundamental; breaking people down into elements or trying to study them as a whole in some sense; seeing them as similar or dissimilar to animals or physical objects . . . The image of people which is formed by taking the first series of options in this dichotomy is of passive creatures whose behaviour is uniform, controllable and predictable. The second series of options reveals creatures who are active, free and who can radically alter their patterns of behaviour. Behaviourist psychology has tended to take the first options . . . the second options . . . have yielded functionalist, introspective, Gestalt, phenomenological, existentialist and developmental psychologies.[21]

Finally, by viewing theories of human nature as a product, rather than a precondition, of the social sciences, educational philosophers have overlooked the extent to which many moral philosophers are agreed that the choice of a theory of human nature is always influenced by moral beliefs and concerns, and conversely, that moral beliefs and concerns are always determined by a theory of human nature.[22] This is so because theories of human nature always suggest beliefs about those human needs which ought to be satisfied. But since it is such beliefs that partly determine moral beliefs, and since moral beliefs provide the criteria in terms of which theories of human nature are chosen, it follows that 'the choice of morality and the choice of a view of human nature go together'.[23] Hence, a theory of human nature is partly determined by a moral outlook and how a moral outlook is justified is partly determined by a theory of human nature.

The collective significance of these philosophical insights can be summarized like this. Although traditional educational philosophy seeks to support educational values by appealing to metaphysical assumptions about human nature, this should not obscure the way in which precisely the same kind of assumptions support the explanations of the social sciences. Moreover, since theories of human nature imply, and are themselves implied by, moral beliefs, the difference between the social scientific theories used by educational researchers and philosophical theories of education is not that the former are explanatory while the latter are prescriptive. It is simply that while philosophical theories derive normative conclusions from explanatory premises, social scientific theories involve a transition from evaluative premises to explanatory conclusions.

Given these similarities, it is clear that the theories of human nature presupposed by any of the social scientific frameworks used in educational research will operate, just as they do in educational philosophy, to support some conception of educational values and goals. For, just as a view of human nature 'helps to delimit . . . what could be regarded as a morality',[24] so they also help to delimit some conception of what could be regarded as education. This is so for the obvious reason that any conception of education, like any conception of morality, always presupposes the supporting rationale of a theory of human nature.[25] Thus, just as moral beliefs and actions always reflect a view about human nature, so the identification of a practice in terms of its educational value will be justified in the same way. To define a situation as 'educative', to identify a person as 'educated' or to advocate a policy on 'educational grounds' all involve some appeal to criteria of educational value, which, like moral criteria, are partly determined by some conception of human nature.[26]

In the context of the social sciences, a recognition of the metaphysical and moral character of theories of human nature can be employed to examine the precise ways in which political philosophies and philosophies of social science emanating from the same source (e.g. Durkheim, Mannheim, Popper) are logically interdependent and mutually reinforcing.[27] In an educational context, it would be easy enough to apply this kind of examination to those cases where an educational philosophy and a theory of educational research are fixed by the same theory of human nature. Applied, for instance, to the case of B. F. Skinner, this would no doubt clarify how the view of human nature underpinning his theory of psychology justifies and is itself justified by the view or morality expounded in *Beyond Freedom and Dignity*. The recognition of this logical relationship between Skinner's moral beliefs and his theory of psychology could then be extended to show why this always implies a similar relationship between his educational philosophy and behaviourism as a form of educational research. This, in turn, would make it clear that both the behaviourist model of educational research and Skinner's educational philosophy depend on the view of morality supporting and supported by his theory of human nature. It would then be self-evident to any educational researchers prepared to be reflective about the philosophical foundations of their work that, in the very act of adopting a behaviourist approach to research, they thereby committed themselves to a Skinnerian conception of the nature and value of education.

What, so far, I have argued is that the metaphysical theories of human nature which are explicit in educational philosophies are also implicit in the methodological frameworks employed in educational research and that such theories always embody a conception of educational values. It follows from this that the choice of an approach to educational research always implies a preference for the theory of human nature on which it is based, and a commitment to the particular educational values it sustains. The writer who has done most to clarify the range of value-choices available in social scientific research is Jürgen Habermas. Since the appearance of his *Knowledge and Human Interests*[28] it has been generally acknowledged that there are three possible ways of conceptualizing social scientific research, each based on a different understanding of the kind of 'human interests' that knowledge of social life serves. Habermas calls these the 'empirical-analytic sciences', based on instrumental

Table 6.1

	Empirical analytic	Historical hermeneutic	Critical
Research methods	Natural scientific; experimental; quantitative	Historical interpretive; ethno-methodological; illuminative;	Critical social science; emancipatory action-research
Form of research knowledge	Objective; nomological; explanatory theories	Subjective; ideographic; interpretive understandings	Dialectical; reflexive understanding; 'praxis'
Human interest	Technical	Practical	Emancipatory
Practical purpose	Instrumental: 'means–end'	Deliberative: informs judgement	Critical: transformative
Theories of human nature	Deterministic	Humanistic	Historical
Educational philosophies	Neo-classical	Liberal progressive	Socially critical
Educational values	'Moulding' metaphor: individuals prepared for a given form of social life	'Growth' metaphor: self-actualization of individuals in a meritocratic form of social life	'Empowerment' metaphor: individuals as producing and transforming a given form of social life

values and a 'technical' interest in manipulation and control; the 'historical or hermeneutic sciences', based on the values of open dialogue and the 'practical interest' in free communication; and 'critical sciences' which serve the 'emancipatory' interest of eliminating the social and political constraints which distort rational self-understanding.[29] What, for present purposes, is important about Habermas's 'theory of knowledge constitutive interests' is the way in which it helps to clarify how the values which constitute different forms of social scientific knowledge also express different philosophical views about the nature of education itself. These views can be made explicit by relating the methods, knowledge and interests characteristic of three alternative styles of educational research to three general philosophical traditions through which different educational values are sustained. These relationships can be set out as in Table 6.1.

Closer examination of these relationships could, no doubt, develop along the lines of similar examinations of the connections between political values and particular forms of social science.[30] However, once such relationships are recognized, any idea that research methods can be assessed solely on the basis of their theoretical virtues becomes inadmissible. The choice of a research stance is never just the reflection of an intellectual preference, it always embodies an educational commitment as well.[31]

A recognition of these relationships also makes it clear that attempts to use research strategies that are infused by one set of educational values to study educational practices that are infused by another is, to say the least, misleading. When this happens (for example, when teaching methods designed to foster and promote the educational values of a 'liberal-progressive' philosophy are assessed through 'empirical-analytic' research methods), the results should not be taken too seriously. These results are not so much objective scientific knowledge as the predictable outcome of the educational values in terms of which the research was conducted.

Although I have emphasized the need for educational researchers to make choices about educational philosophies and values, this does not itself imply a particular preference for one research approach rather than any other. What it does imply, however, is that the conventional assumption that educational research can only be accepted as a genuine science if it adopts the 'value-free' methods of the empirical-analytic sciences, is no longer justifiable. This brings me to my final claim, which is that philosophy and values will necessarily feature in any contemporary account of an educational science.

IV

There are many standard arguments for supposing that educational research cannot be modelled on the natural sciences[32] and, conversely, for supposing that the methods of educational research and natural science are, or ought to be, the same.[33] Most of these arguments are unsatisfactory for at least two reasons. First, they tend to conflate *naturalism* (the claim that social science can replicate the structure of natural scientific reasoning) with either *scientism* (the claim that the methods of the natural and social sciences are not significantly different) or *reductionism* (the claim that the subject matter of the natural and social sciences is basically the same). Second, the conventional arguments tend to ignore the extent to which answers to questions about the scientific status of educational research always depend on some philosophical view about the nature of science itself. For example, the widespread belief that educational research can only be scientific if it is value-free presumes an empiricist philosophy of science, with its image of scientific research as involving the use of impersonal deductive logic to test hypotheses against empirical observations.[34]

Despite its continuing popularity among educational researchers, empiricist philosophy has so persistently failed to provide an adequate epistemology for the natural sciences that 'it is now almost universally discredited'.[35] What contributed to, and developed from, the demise of empiricism was a set of interrelated ideas and arguments which together constitute what has become known as the 'post-empiricist' philosophy of science.[36] Some of the familiar and uncontroversial theses on which this alternative philosophy of science have been erected are as follows.[37]

1 *Science is empirical.* To label a study 'scientific' implies that its knowledge claims are empirically testable.[38]
2 *Scientific theories are empirically under-determined.* Although scientific theories are empirically constrained, they can be neither conclusively verified nor conclusively refuted by experience alone. Hence, since they are empirically

under-determined, the choice of scientific theories always requires an appeal to extra, non-empirical criteria.[39]

3 *Observation statements are theory-laden.* The reason why scientific theories cannot be empirically determined is that there is no theory-free language for reporting empirical observations. Observation statements always employ concepts which interpret empirical phenomena in accordance with some logically prior theoretical scheme. Hence, theoretical and empirical concepts cannot be radically separated.[40]

4 *Scientific inquiries are governed by 'research programmes'.* The theoretical context presupposed by any scientific inquiry is provided by the 'research programme' to which those engaged in this inquiry are committed. Scientific progress and scientific innovation are not, therefore, the results of a disinterested search for knowledge. Rather, science develops by successfully confronting the 'problem situations' which the 'positive heuristic' of a 'research programme' stimulates.[41]

5 *Science has metaphysical foundations.* A research programme emanates from some overall 'paradigm' which incorporates a metaphysically inspired 'world view'. Hence, science always operates on metaphysical assumptions which are not themselves amenable to explanation through scientific research. On the contrary, they provide the 'interpretation of reality' which any model of scientific research and any notion of scientific explanation always presuppose.[42]

One of the outstanding tasks for this post-empiricist account of science is to resolve the obvious tensions between its claims that scientific theories are empirically under-determined (thesis 2) yet in some sense empirically testable (thesis 1).[43] However, despite this and other difficulties, there is now little doubt that this 'new philosophy of science' constitutes a significant advance over traditional empiricism and generates an image of science which is far superior to the hypothetico-deductive model it has now replaced. It also makes it abundantly clear that many of the conventional arguments about the role of philosophy and values in any educational science are now obsolete. For example, since it is now recognized that the theoretical frameworks of the natural sciences have metaphysical foundations (thesis 5), the fact that educational research presupposes metaphysical assumptions about human nature is no impediment to its scientific status. All that needs to be recognized is that because the metaphysical elements of an educational science include a theory of human nature, an educational science will promote not only certain kinds of explanation but certain kinds of educational values as well.

Second, because theoretical and empirical statements cannot be sharply separated (thesis 3), attempts to confine educational values to a separate realm of 'philosophical' assumptions and exclude them from the area of 'empirical' research are inadmissible. Theory choice ('the context of discovery') and theory testing ('the context of justification') are indissoluble parts of one whole, not independent or separate domains. In so far as conventional arguments about the scientific status of educational research assume otherwise, they operate on the basis of an unintegrated, and now discredited, empiricist philosophy of science.

Of greater significance, however, is the way in which this 'new' philosophy of science suggests the outlines of an educational science in which philosophy and values are seen as integral rather than antithetical. Thus, just as post-empiricism makes clear that the problems of natural scientific research are selected in response to a particular 'research programme' (thesis 5), so it suggests that the problems of any educational science should be determined in the same way. The only difference is that while the 'research programme' of a natural science represents a prior commitment to some philosophical view of 'the nature of reality', that of an educational science represents a prior commitment to a philosophical view of the nature of education. While the research problems of a natural science stem from discrepancies between its philosophical picture of reality and concrete reality itself, the research problems of an educational science reflect the discrepancies between the educational philosophy it seeks to foster and the actual educational practices through which it is being expressed. Hence, while a natural scientific 'research programme' always operates with philosophical preconceptions about what *is* the case, that of an educational science always operates with philosophical preconceptions about what *ought to be* the case.

Similarly, since scientific theories are always under-determined by empirical constraints (thesis 2), an educational science will, like any natural science, appeal to extra, non-empirical criteria in the exercise of theory choice. In the natural sciences these non-empirical criteria are provided by 'pragmatic values' concerned with the goal of 'increasingly successful prediction and control of the environment'.[44] What is distinctive of any *educational* science is that it self-consciously appeals to *educational* values as a further criterion of theory acceptability and choice. Thus, while the under-determination thesis entails that *all* genuine sciences exercise some discretion in deciding which theoretical framework to adopt, the hallmark of any *educational* science is that it takes up this option by reference to the different educational values that competing research approaches sustain.

Although this account suggests how value-laden educational research may be scientific in the same *sense* as the natural sciences, this does not imply that it will be scientific in the same *way* as the natural sciences. It is therefore neither reductionist nor scientistic. On the contrary, it implies that, precisely because of its distinctive problems and subject matter, any educational science will require different methods from those of the natural sciences and will develop in a very different way. For example, it would be a scientistic error to believe that educational research can only advance its scientific prospects by adopting the 'objective' standpoint of the natural sciences. This is not simply to say that objectivity is an ideal which is virtually unattainable in educational research. Rather, it is to say that because educational research always involves a positive commitment to educational values, the pursuit of objectivity as understood in the natural sciences is undesirable.

Similarly, any idea that the variety of approaches and methods now being used in educational research is a sign of its 'immature' or 'pre-paradigmatic' state of development is a reductionist mistake. So too is any suggestion that the development of an educational science requires the identification of some logical ground rules for adjudicating in methodological disputes. No such rules can be identified because these disputes do not reflect theoretical immaturity or logical confusion so much as disagreements about the kind of educational values researchers ought to adopt. Moreover, since the non-empirical criteria of theory choice available to educational researchers will be as diverse as the range of educational values they are prepared to accept, and since these values are themselves always indeterminate and contestable, the theory choices of educational researchers can be no more determined by a single set of educational values than by purely theoretical or empirical considerations. Educational research is, no less than education itself, an essentially contested terrain. The elimination of methodological diversity and the emergence of a single method of educational research would therefore not be indicative of scientific maturity but of a research community in which disagreement about educational values had disappeared or been suppressed.

Clearly, the argument that educational research may be both value-laden and scientific would benefit from close inspection of philosophical arguments designed to sustain this view of social scientific inquiry generally.[45] It is also clear that the argument would be more readily accessible if it was more closely informed by attempts to devise research strategies explicitly concerned with the promotion of educational values.[46] However, the attraction of an educational science understood in these terms is already apparent. For it foreshadows a view of educational research as a genuine 'moral science' in which the relevance of both normative and empirical considerations is given full recognition.[47] As such, it anticipates the emergence of a form of educational research which denies the 'scientific' character of philosophical theories in which empirical content simply serves illustrative purposes and, at the same time, denies the 'educational' character of empirical studies which are uncommitted to the realization of educational values and goals.

V

Three conclusions. First, if I am correct in supposing values to be an inescapable category in educational research, then, once again, the old positivist segregation of facts and values breaks down. Educational researchers are committed to values simply by virtue of engaging in their work.

Second, since educational researchers cannot evade the task of deciding the educational values appropriate to their work, they cannot evade the responsibility for critically examining and justifying the educational values that their inquiries seek to foster and promote. But since to do this is to engage in philosophy, it follows that philosophical reflection and argumentation are central features of the methods and procedures of research. The expulsion of educational philosophy from educational research – or at least its confinement to the task of analysing research concepts and methodologies – turns out to be yet another positivist mistake.

Third, philosophy and values are not just a necessary but inconvenient feature of educational research; they are an indispensable requirement for the development of any genuinely educational science. Indeed it is only by virtue of a self-conscious desire to be guided and informed by philosophical beliefs about the value of education that the educational character of any phenomena can be recognized and the educational qualities of any research sustained. It is somewhat ironical that the educational values which positivism construes as a major weakness in the case for an educational science turn out to be its major source of strength.

If these conclusions are taken seriously, then educational research can no longer confine itself to the official discourse of a 'value-free' theoretical discipline. Rather must it seek to articulate and examine the relationship between the educational realities it purports to explain and the educational values it unavoidably defends and promotes. This does not mean that educational research has to abandon its aspirations to become a legitimate scientific pursuit. What has to be abandoned is the desire to define educational research in accordance with a discredited notion of scientific purity and in conformity with existing divisions between non-philosophical empirical science and non-empirical philosophical inquiry. When this happens, the claim that educational research has now been rescued from philosophy and values will no longer be regarded as an indication of methodological progress, but as one of the illusions of the present age.

7 WHATEVER HAPPENED

TO ACTION

RESEARCH?

The positive mind no longer asks why, ceases to speculate on
the hidden nature of things. It asks how phenomena arise
and what course they take, it collects facts and is ready to
submit to facts, it subjects thinking to the continuous
control of 'objective facts'.[1]

The title of this chapter is also the title of a paper Nevitt Sanford presented to
an audience of American social psychologists in 1970.[2] In his paper, Sanford
described how the term 'action research' had first come to prominence in
America through the work of Kurt Lewin in the 1940s and how it was taken up
and developed by a large number of social scientists who recognized that social
problems could only be adequately resolved if theory and practice (action and
research) were developed together.[3] In assessing the American experience of
trying to put Lewin's ideas into effect, Sanford had to concede that, despite a
good deal of activity, 'action research never really got off the ground'.[4] The
main reason for this, he argued, was that action research had allowed itself to
become institutionalized in a way which virtually ensured that it could not
meet the challenges to which it was initially a response (the conservatism and
elitism of academia, the theoretical orientation of conventional social research, the increasing technologization of social life). Indeed, Sanford argued,
the institutionalization of action research meant that Lewin's original idea had
to be modified so that it could be accommodated within the social science
establishment – an establishment which, as Sanford noted, 'was part of the
larger political and economic establishment . . . upon which it depended for
support'.[5] Once action research had been taken over by the academic establishment, it was only a matter of time before it was reinterpreted from the

perspective of the dominant positivist research paradigm and repackaged as little more than a set of practical problem solving techniques. 'Whatever happened to action research?' Sanford summarized his assessment in the following way:

I would say now that action-research never really got off the ground, it never was widely influential . . . After World War II the separation of science and practice was institutionalised and it has been so ever since . . . I would say that we have separated – and institutionalised the separation – of everything that – from the point of view of action research . . . belong together.[6]

The cultural and intellectual context in which action research resurfaced in Britain in the 1970s was, of course, very different from that of its American predecessor. The positivist paradigm, which had dominated American social research in the 1940s and 1950s was widely rejected – both for its theoretical weaknesses and for its perceived irrelevance to the practical problems of social life. In education, the major response to positivism's theoretical defects was a resurgence of interest in the interpretive tradition of social inquiry. The major responses to positivism's practical impotence was Lawrence Stenhouse's compelling image of the 'teacher-as-researcher' and the subsequent introduction of a reformulated view of action research.[7]

The view of educational action research which emerged in Britain in the 1970s was thus significantly different from its American forerunner. Intellectually, it was sympathetic to 'naturalistic' and 'case study' methodologies, with their emphasis on the perspectives of participants and social actors. Educationally, it endorsed humanistic values and construed teaching and learning as processes through which these values were to be realized. Revived and revised in this way, British educational action research could be presented as a form of inquiry which enabled teachers to clarify and develop their educational values through systematic reflection on their classroom practice. And, revived and revised in this way, action research held out the promise that, this time, it would escape the positivist distortions that had thwarted its American predecessor. The key question is: has it succeeded?

When, in 1978, John Elliott published 'What is action research in schools?',[8] British educational research was still dominated by positivist distinctions between research and action, knowing and doing, theory and practice. And these conceptual distinctions still supported an institutionalized division of labour which portrayed teachers as theoretically impoverished and made educational research the exclusive preserve of an academic elite. What made Elliott's description of action research so compelling was that it interpreted teaching as ineradicably theoretical and defined research as a self-reflective process in which teachers examined the theories implicit in their own everyday practice. Described in this way, action research promised a reunification of theory and practice which would eliminate the segregation of teaching and research which positivism has created and sustained.

With hindsight, it is now obvious that Elliott was introducing an idea whose time had come. In the ensuing decade, action research was to become nothing less than a full blown 'movement' sustained by a large number of teachers, teacher educators and educational researchers and supported by numerous educational institutions and research agencies in Britain, Australia, continental Europe and the USA. As a result, the next ten years witnessed the emergence of local action research 'networks',[9] the funding of several major action research projects[10] and the publication of a steady stream of books explaining the action research method and offering teachers advice about how it can be used.[11] However, this enthusiasm for a research paradigm aimed at developing teachers' practical understanding was not always matched by a similar enthusiasm for developing a more refined theoretical understanding of how action research is to be interpreted and understood.[12] Action research now means different things to different people and, as a result, the action research movement often appears to be held together by little more than a common contempt for academic theorizing and a general disenchantment with 'mainstream' research. Everybody knows what action research is against. But the important and still unresolved question is: what is it for?

Evidence for supposing that this question may not be receiving the kind of attention that it should is not hard to find. Certainly, nobody could claim that the steady flow of books that have now been published on action research are bound together by a positive allegiance to some unifying idea. On the contrary, they display a multiplicity of views about the practical purposes of action research and interpret its meaning and significance in different, and sometimes incompatible, ways. Some regard action research primarily as a way of deepening teachers' understanding while others stress its role in stimulating practical improvement and change. Yet others see action research as an effective way of communicating research findings to teachers. For some, action research is a way of making teachers' professional knowledge more explicit; for others, it is a way of making teachers' professional knowledge more objective. The editors of one book have openly acknowledged that their own 'eclectic' interpretation of action research 'will be seen to beg the question of hard definition by many action researchers who have taken a stand on what action research is really all about'.[13] But the fact remains that the general reluctance of the action research movement to take such a stand means that action research still lacks any coherent theoretical rationale and so can be defended only rhetorically and pragmatically. Because of this, traditional educational researchers can easily reject action research's claims to intellectual respectability and teachers can easily dismiss its claims to offer them a means for improving their practice as idealistic nonsense. If the modern action research movement is to escape the fate of its American predecessor then, clearly, it must develop the kind of theoretical self-understanding that would enable it to repudiate these criticisms and facilitate its future progress.

One action researcher who has tried to develop this kind of self-understanding is Richard Winter. In two books – *Action Research and the Nature of Social Inquiry*[14] and *Learning from Experience: Principles and Practice in Action Research*[15] – Winter argues that action research should be seen not just as a methodological device for solving the practical problem of relating research to practical change, but, more importantly, as a source of fundamental theoretical problems about how this relationship is to be understood. The way in which the action research movement currently understands this relationship continues to be conditioned by inherited positivist distinctions – such as those between 'action' and 'research', 'general' and 'particular', 'common-sense understanding' and 'academic expertise'. For Winter, the appeal of action research resides entirely in its claim to be able to transcend these distinctions in a way which will make the epistemological and institutional reunification of theory and practice a real possibility. Thus, in *Action Research and the Nature of Social Inquiry* he takes as his starting point precisely those questions which most action researchers take care to avoid. What is the legitimate nature of action research? What criteria should be used to judge claims to be engaged in action research? What kind of philosophical insights and conceptual resources are available for establishing its validity? 'The aim of the study', says Winter, 'is to provide an analytic theory of action research, a set of conditions for its theoretic possibility.'[16]

Winter's strategy for uncovering these conditions is to appeal to two fundamental principles: that the relationship between 'action' and 'research' has to be grasped *dialectically*; and that action research can only offer a genuine alternative to positivism by more fully acknowledging the importance of *reflexivity* for its own mode of inquiry. Sustained by these two principles, Winter moves towards a form of action research understood primarily as a reflexive and dialectical process of critique: a process which does not eschew 'theory' in order to improve 'practice' but which preserves the dialectical unity of theory and practice by understanding them as mutually constitutive elements in a dynamic, developing and integrated whole. Thus, for Winter, action research is a form of inquiry which seeks to reveal to teachers the transient and contingent status of their practice in a way which makes it amenable to critical transformation. In order to do this, he argues that action research must endorse an epistemology which treats rationality as critical and dialectical. Informed by this kind of epistemology, action research would be primarily concerned with enabling teachers to reflect critically on the contradictions between their educational ideas and beliefs and the institutionalized practices through which these ideas and beliefs are expressed. Thus Winter concludes:

> What a reflexive action-research would offer . . . is not 'theory' . . . It would propose, rather, to subject the theories of common-sense and of professional expertise to a critical analysis of their located-ness within the practice whose intelligibility they serve. Action research thus proposes a move 'beyond' theories . . . which prescribe and justify an interpretive basis for action towards a reflexive awareness of the dialectic which can sustain their mutuality while transforming both.[17]

Action Research and the Nature of Social Inquiry is a fine book and it is a pity that Winter found it necessary to couch his argument in highly abstract and dense prose and so run the risk of producing just that kind of 'theoretical treatise' which many action researchers choose to ignore. But the main value of Winter's book has little to do with how its argument is expressed. It is that it helps to clarify a number of neglected questions about the way in which the action research movement has developed in recent years – questions which some action researchers would no doubt dismiss as prime examples of the kind of sterile 'academic' theorizing which has little to do with the practical conduct of their work.

Many of these questions stem from the fact that action research is faced with a danger which, if Thomas Kuhn is to be believed, threatens all attempts to popularize a radically new research paradigm. For such a paradigm to advance, its advocates are forced to justify its claims to superiority by using the language and evaluative standards which some pre-existing paradigm has already supplied. As it becomes more widely established, there is, therefore, always the risk that the original aspirations of the new paradigm will be dissipated and its original meaning surreptitiously reinterpreted so as to accommodate more continuities with its predecessor than it was initially prepared to admit. It goes without saying that, when this happens, the price paid for the successful advancement of the new paradigm will have been to reduce it from a full-blown alternative view of the nature of 'research' to a set of ideas and methods which can be accommodated within the broad requirements of the very paradigm it had originally promised to eliminate and replace.

Does this kind of scenario offer any useful warnings about the way in which educational action research has developed? Despite its theoretical claim to offer a radical alternative to positivist research, does action research, in practice, display a tendency to relapse into old positivist ways? The suspicion that it does is hardly dispelled by the numerous portrayals of action research as a form of conventional research suitable for ordinary teachers. And it is positively reinforced by numerous examples of action research literature which display more than a modicum of positivist thought. But is it true that action research is in danger of becoming little more than a sophisticated form of positivism?

A necessary prerequisite to any proper discussion of this question is to recognize that action research still lacks an adequate analysis of its own relationship to positivism, and hence that this relationship is still ambiguous and confused. Some of these confusions stem from the fact that the term 'positivism' now frequently functions as little more than a derogatory label or a term of abuse. But most of them stem from a general failure to appreciate that many of the dangers currently threatening the future of action research can only be understood by understanding some of the key episodes in the history of positivist thought.

One such episode concerns the origins of positivism. What we now refer to as 'positivist' doctrines have their roots in an all-pervading intellectual and moral outlook which began to dominate Western thought in the latter half of the nineteenth century.[18] One of the prominent characteristics of this outlook was a deep-seated aversion to philosophical thinking and a firm insistence that only neutral 'experience' could provide an acceptable foundation for valid knowledge. It is thus unsurprising to find that, throughout its long history, the common aim of various positivist movements – whether in history, morality, politics or the social sciences – has been to offer a dispensation from any obligation to engage in critical or reflective thought. One measure of the extent to which positivism has achieved this aim is its success in denying reflectively acquired self-knowledge as a valid epistemological category. Another is its success in excluding all those forms of social and educational theorizing which refuse to confine themselves to experience 'as it is' but instead insist that experience is always conditioned by philosophical interpretation and historical understanding. It is thus no accident that modern positivist methodologies offer an escape from troublesome philosophical questions and legitimate an indifference to major social, political and moral concerns. It is also no accident that positivist research flourishes in those cultures which treat philosophy and history as academic pastimes that can easily be dismissed and ignored.

A second salient feature of positivism's history concerns its changing cultural role. What is particularly important to note is how, in the transition from the social context in which it has its origins to our own contemporary culture, 'positivism' has been transformed from a critically examined and culturally subversive set of radical arguments into a uncritically accepted and culturally supported set of common-sense assumptions which penetrate all aspects of social life. Ironically, the intricate theoretical ideas advanced by nineteenth-century positivists, on the grounds that they offered a true understanding of how ideology was to be expunged from social life, themselves now serve a central ideological role in maintaining dominant forms of social life. It is for this reason that positivist principles that are consistently and conclusively refuted at the level of philosophical theory continue to exercise a decisive influence on contemporary educational policy and practice. Indeed, one important way of understanding the ideological role now played by positivism is to note the extent to which educational theorists, researchers, policy-makers and practitioners – irrespective of their self-consciously proclaimed theoretical positions or educational ideals – now talk, think and act in ways which presume certain positivist assumptions to be true.

Thus, once positivism is considered historically, it becomes increasingly clear that it cannot be eliminated or dismissed in the easy, confident manner that some action researchers seem to suggest. Action research has to confront positivism not just as a theory of knowledge but as a theory embedded in social life and hence in the discourse, organization and practice of education as well. Positivism's central assumptions – about theory and knowledge, subjectivity and objectivity, facts and values – are not just to be found in textbook descriptions of educational research. They also appear as a set of educational practices which are grounded in everyday language and experience and are implicit in the institutionalized social relationships governing the organization of education and educational research. Action researchers who complain about positivist research usually do so as members of institutions which serve to perpetuate it. And action researchers who complain about the institutional constraints on their work often fail to notice that these constraints are just as much a legacy of positivism as is the inherited theoretical discourse of conventional educational research.

What the history of positivism makes equally clear is that, although action research offers itself as a radical alternative to positivism, there are some disturbing similarities between the two. For example, action research retains positivism's distrust of philosophy. It does so not in the obvious sense of displaying an open hostility to philosophical theories, but in the less obvious sense of conforming to the positivist axiom that 'research' is a systematic and methodical process for acquiring positive knowledge rather than a dialogical and reflective process of democratic discussion and philosophical critique. The modern separation of 'philosophical critique' from 'methodical inquiry' (and the subsequent deformation of both) is one of positivism's most enduring ideological achievements. It is strengthened, rather than challenged, by the way in which action research presents itself as a method which is largely devoid of philosophical assumptions and interpretations. It is further reinforced by the willingness of action researchers to give due recognition to those methodological strategies (the systematic collection and analysis of data etc.) which were initially designed to insulate inquiry from philosophical intrusion.[19] It is scarcely surprising therefore that many action researchers' interpretation of 'research' is that which positivism has vindicated, and that their view of 'positivism' is that vindicated by research so understood. The mistake underlying these mutually confirming interpretations is, of course, that of supposing that there can be a philosophically uncontested, ahistorical concept of 'research' – an illusion which an understanding of the history of positivism would immediately dispel. While it lacks this kind of historical understanding, action research will continue to run the risk of confusing the concept of research as such with the concept of research as interpreted in positivist terms.

Some of the other positivist tendencies displayed by contemporary action research can be rapidly stated. Much of what now passes for action research embraces an asocial view of 'action', clings to a rationalistic notion of 'theory', employs a narrow view of the role of 'criticism' and pays lip service to the importance of the concept of 'self-reflection' without adequately appreciating its profound importance for the question of what action research is and what it is not. In theory, action research is only intelligible as an attempt to revive those forms of democratic dialogue and reflective theorizing which, under the impact of positivism, have been rendered marginal. But, in practice, action research increasingly conveys an image of itself as a research method which is favourable to the ideas of methodological sophistication and technical proficiency but which remains unable to provide the idea of critical self-reflection with any genuine practical expression. Because of this discrepancy between its own theoretically conceived guiding ideals and its socially embedded institutionalized practice, action research may be falling victim to the very theory–practice dualism it initially aspired to overcome. This should serve to remind us of one more feature of positivism's history.

The positivist movement began by proclaiming a way of relating theory to practice that would free us from all those authoritative forms of 'academic' theorizing which were unconstrained by the real world of 'experience'. In this sense, positivism was, in its own terms, nothing other than a nineteenth-century precursor of modern action research. Both were driven by a desire to liberate ordinary practical thought and action from the dogmatically imposed theories of 'authoritative experts'. And it was their optimistic faith in the power of experience-based knowledge to solve practical problems which gave them both their initial attraction and appeal. Of course, as positivism's initial promise remained unrealized, so its association with the ideals of intellectual freedom and practical progress have now given way to an association with intellectual constraint and practical control. It goes without saying that the high-minded and enlightened positivists of the nineteenth century did not in the slightest degree recommend that their ideas and theories should have these associations. Rather is it the case that this is what positivism had to become when elaborated in terms of the dominant values, attitudes and beliefs which constitute twentieth-century human culture.

Whatever happened to action research? What I have tried to show is that if British action research is to avoid the fate of its American predecessor then it has to concede that the present condition of educational action research will be misunderstood if we look for explanations of this condition only in action research's own internal history. But once we are prepared to place the recent history of educational action research in a much longer and larger history of intellectual inquiry, and once we are prepared to admit that the history of intellectual inquiry cannot be abstracted from social and cultural history generally, then we shall begin to understand why action research may yet become a twentieth-century re-enactment of nineteenth-century positivism.

8 THE IDEA OF AN EDUCATIONAL SCIENCE

If you want schools to perpetuate the present order with
such additions as enable it to do better what it is already
doing . . . then one type of intellectual method or 'science' is
indicated. But if one conceives that a social order different in
quality and direction from the present is desirable and that
schools should strive to educate with social change in view
by producing individuals not complacent about what already
exists, and equipped with desires and abilities to assist in
transforming it, quite a different content and method is
indicated for educational science.[1]

I

'No one, I suppose', wrote D. J. O'Connor, 'believes that education is itself a
science . . . It is rather a set of practical activities which provide the focus for
the application of various sciences.'[2] It is indicative of the power of the
British empiricist tradition that this 'applied science' view of education is
rarely challenged or opposed. On this view, 'science' is one thing, 'education' is something else. Science is a value-free theoretical activity concerned
only with the disinterested pursuit of empirical knowledge; education is a
value-loaded practical activity concerned with promoting human values and
social ideals. Here, as elsewhere, empiricism imposes its rigid dualisms between facts and values, knowledge and action, theory and practice. And
here, as elsewhere, these conceptual distinctions support an institutionalized
division of labour based on an ideology of expertise. It is thus to the professional scientist that O'Connor reserves the right 'to produce explanations of

the workings of the educational process'.[3] The task he assigns to the educational practitioner is simply to put this explanatory scientific knowledge to effective practical use.

During the past twenty years, the philosophical basis of this view of science has been 'universally discredited'[4] and replaced by a 'post-empiricist philosophy of science' which renders the traditional empiricist dualisms largely untenable.[5] Although the educational implications of post-empiricist philosophy of science are far reaching, I do not intend to consider them here.[6] Instead, I intend to explore the idea of an educational science which does not appeal solely to philosophical arguments about the nature and purpose of science, but also draws on philosophical arguments about the nature and purpose of education itself. The central concern of this chapter is thus with the idea of an educational science which is rooted in a general philosophy of education rather than a specific philosophy of science.

No doubt the suggestion that an educational science can rest its claims to legitimacy on an educational philosophy will cause considerable confusion and unease. How can an educational philosophy provide the intellectual foundation for an educational science? Surely, an educational science requires a philosophical justification of what constitutes valid knowledge *about* education rather than a philosophical justification for education itself. In order to respond to these questions I have divided this chapter into four parts. First, I shall describe a traditional and long-standing view of education in a way which clarifies the philosophical assumptions on which it rests. Second, I shall seek to show that, when elaborated in the context of contemporary social theory, these philosophical assumptions provide the foundations for a particular form of science. Third, I shall try to defend the idea of an educational science which is 'educational' because it incorporates a view of science informed by precisely those philosophical assumptions that inform our traditional conception of education. Finally, by contrasting this version of an educational science with the more conventional empiricist version, I shall identify its salient characteristics and describe some of the conditions necessary for its practical realization.

II

In his famous essay *On Liberty*, J. S. Mill argued that:

> the free development of individuality is one of the leading essentials of well-being. It is . . . the proper condition of a human being . . . to use and interpret experience in his own way . . . To conform to custom, merely *as* custom, does not educate or develop in him any of the qualities which are the distinctive endowment of a human being. The human facilities of perception, judgement, discriminate feeling, mental activity and even moral preference, are exercised only in making a choice . . . Human nature is not a machine to be built after a model, and set to do exactly the work prescribed for it, but a tree which requires to grow and develop on all sides.[7]

Here Mill offers an argument for a view of education which has been a persistent feature of our Western intellectual tradition. According to this view, education is intimately concerned with promoting human freedom by developing the innate capacities of individuals to think for themselves: to deliberate, judge and choose on the basis of their own rational reflections. It is a view of education which has its origins in the Greek desire to distinguish a form of education conducive to the general empowering of the rational mind from more mundane attempts to instil instrumental knowledge or specialist skills. Its most influential exposition is still to be found in Plato's *Republic*, but its more modern formulations have their roots in the eighteenth-century philosophy of Enlightenment – a philosophy which received its clearest expression in Kant's demand for the liberation of human reason and the rational 'enlightenment' of human thought.[8]

Consider now some of the shared assumptions to which exponents of Enlightenment educational philosophies invariably subscribe. First, all assume that individuals *qua* human beings cannot be understood in isolation from the society of which they are a part. To be human is to have acquired the concepts, language and modes of self-understanding embedded in a particular form of social life. Conversely, a particular form of social life is partially defined by the shared network of concepts and modes of discourse which individuals employ in understanding themselves and the ways in which they live. On this view, the idea of the individual as existing prior to, or separate from, society is just as incoherent as the idea of society as some kind of objective entity existing without the intervention of human activity or purpose. Individuals and society are dialectically related; each is constituted by, and constitutive of, the other.

But, as well as being social animals, human beings are also rational animals who are able to use their powers of reason to reflect critically upon their conceptions of themselves and their shared forms of social life. Thus, a second shared assumption is that what is distinctive of human beings is their capacity to reason: the universal capacity of all people to reflect rationally on the sense of themselves that they have already acquired, to consider whether this inherited self-understanding is conducive to the promotion of their needs and interests and, on the basis of such rational knowledge, to transform themselves and their social world. Hence, a third common characteristic of Enlightenment educational philosophies is a commitment to the aims and values associated with the development of rational autonomy – aims and values which, historically, have been articulated in a variety of different ways but which always reflect the view that, through education, individuals may become emancipated from the dictates of ignorance and superstition and so become rationally empowered to transform themselves and the social world in which they live. Of course, those subscribing to Enlightenment educational philosophies recognized that the educational aim of rational autonomy can only be realistically pursued in a society which has itself institutionalized the principles of rational justification – a society which permits freedom of thought and speech and in which all can participate in debate free from irrational constraints and controls. Thus a fourth feature of Enlightenment educational philosophies is that they invariably seek to defend and promote the development of a democratic society in which all individuals are able to exercise their powers of rational thought.

The most influential modern exponent of this Enlightenment view of education has undoubtedly been R. S. Peters.[9] Indeed, in many ways, Peters's educational philosophy may be read as a sustained attempt to protect this concept of education from the kind of instrumental thinking which now tends to dominate modern educational thought. Like his predecessors, Peters asserts that reason is central to any conception of human nature[10] and that the development of rational autonomy is a fundamental educational aim. And, like his predecessors, Peters insists that the freedom rationally to determine one's own beliefs and actions always presupposes a freedom from any social influences or cultural constraints which may impede the development of autonomous rational thought.[11] For education to promote rational autonomy, Peters argues,[12] it must help individuals to understand themselves as both the producers and the products of their social world. By enabling individuals to recognize themselves in society, he maintains, education helps them to 'purge' their thinking of 'irrational allegiances' and so to transform their understanding of 'the human condition'. Peters eloquently portrays this Enlightenment view of education in the following way:

> The individual brings to his experience a stock of beliefs, attitudes and expectations. Most of these rest on authority . . . Many of them are erroneous, prejudiced and simple-minded, especially in the political realms where evidence shows that opinions depend overwhelmingly on traditional and irrational allegiances. One of the aims of education is to make them less so . . . The individual can improve his understanding and purge his beliefs and attitudes by ridding them of error, superstition and prejudice. And, through the development of understanding, he can come to view the human condition in a very different light. New opportunities for action may open up as his view of people, society and the natural world changes . . . and he may be fired by the thought of participating in the change of institutions, that he had previously regarded as fixed points in his social world.[13]

The reason for drawing attention to Peters's educational philosophy is not solely to emphasize its importance in maintaining the validity of the Enlightenment concept of education. It is also to suggest that it offers important intellectual resources for constructing a form of educational science which employs concepts of knowledge and rationality very different from those supplied by an empiricist philosophy of science. Indeed, implicit in Peter's philosophy is the idea of an educational science that would be 'educational' precisely because it aspired to generate the kind of reflective self-knowledge through which the educational aim of rational autonomy is pursued and achieved.

But how can a form of inquiry which explicitly promotes the Enlightenment ideal of rational autonomy be called a 'science'? How can knowledge arising from a process of self-reflection be called 'scientific'? Fortunately, these questions have been addressed in some detail by contemporary philosophers and social theorists, usually in the context of a wide-ranging discussion about the nature and purpose of the social sciences.[14] One of the most influential attempts to formulate these questions has come from the leading contemporary exponent of critical theory, Jurgen Habermas. 'How', he asks, 'can we reassert the classical ideal of rational self-determination?' 'How are we to recover the forgotten experience of reflection?'[15] But can critical theory provide the intellectual resources for a reconstruction of an educational science based on the aims and values of education itself? Does critical theory have an important role to play in the reconstruction of an *educational* science?

In order to respond to these questions, it will be helpful to consider the differences between two familiar embodiments of the contemporary education scientist. The first, and more easily recognizable, may be labelled 'the Positivist'. Positivist educational scientists believe that objective scientific inquiry can yield true knowledge about education in much the same way that it yields true knowledge about nature. They further assert that their scientific expertise not only entitles them to lay claim to a way of understanding education which is far superior to that of ordinary educational practitioners; it also enables them to discriminate between those educational beliefs of educational practitioners that are rational and those that are not. For the Positivist, then, educational inquiries are simply scientific inquiries designed to improve the rationality of education by purging it of any dependency on irrational dogma or subjective belief.

The second kind of educational scientist may be labelled 'the Marxist'. For the Marxist, positivist educational science is little more than a contrived rationalization for that mode of theoretical discourse which articulates the political and economic interests of a dominant social group. What the Marxist further insists is that the only valid way of understanding education is by recognizing that its primary role is to perpetuate those ideological beliefs which preserve the inequalities and injustices of a capitalist economic order. What the Marxist recommends, therefore, is an approach designed to expose the ideological distortions permeating educational theory and practice and to show how these are largely determined by underlying economic laws.

Normally, the Positivist and the Marxist versions of educational science are sharply opposed but a moment's reflection reveals things to be otherwise. Just as the Positivists can only legitimize their claim to be able to identify irrational or subjective elements in education by appealing to the rationality and objectivity of their own theoretical standpoint, so the Marxists can only justify their claim to be able to detect ideological distorted educational practices in much the same way. If Positivists did not make this claim, there would be no grounds for accepting that they can indeed distinguish those aspects of education which are rational from those which are not. And if the Marxists did not claim for themselves an equally privileged epistemological position, they would be unable to explain why their own thinking was exempt from the ideological contamination they claim to be able to detect in the thinking of others.

Thus, on examination, it turns out that the Marxist and the Positivist versions of educational science are not as opposed as normally believed. What sets them apart is the different theoretical standpoints from which they make their proclamations about the foundations of genuine educational knowledge. But where they are in substantial agreement is in their shared view of educational science as a sophisticated form of theoretical inquiry providing educational knowledge which is much closer to the truth than that possessed by ordinary educational practitioners.

Is this view of educational science sound? Can an educational science only be constructed on the basis of this kind of epistemological elitism? Must the search for an intellectually coherent basis for an educational science always be a choice between those rival versions of how valid educational theories are to be acquired? It is precisely these questions – questions about the practical role of theory – which constitute the core problems of critical theory. Indeed, one way of reading the history of critical theory is as a coherent attempt to reformulate the theory–practice relationship in response to the adverse practical consequences resulting from the rise of positivism and Marxism in the modern world.[16]

The adverse consequences of positivism which most concern critical theory are those resulting from the positivist insistence on treating the social world as epistemologically equivalent to the world of nature. By doing this, positivism has transformed social theorizing into a purely technical activity in which the potential of human reason to generate theories of enlightened action cannot be taken seriously. No longer a form of reflexive thinking aimed at improving the nature and conduct of social life, social inquiry has become a 'value-free' science offering solutions to instrumental problems about how to achieve given practical ends.

What most concerns critical theory about orthodox Marxism is the extent to which it relies on an image of a social world driven by some autonomous 'economic base' over which individuals have no real control. For critical theory, the major consequence of this kind of uncompromising determinism is that it leaves insufficient space for the role of reflexivity in the process of practical change. Like Marxism, critical theory acknowledges that human actions may be socially and ideologically determined. But it does not conclude from this that human actions are either inevitable or unalterable. On the contrary, critical theory insists that the more individuals understand about the social determinants of their actions the more likely they are to escape from the ideological constraints to which they were previously subject.

Thus, for critical theory, the chief threat posed by positivist and Marxist versions of social theory[17] is a threat to one of the central ideals of the Enlightenment: the belief in the capacity of human beings – either as individuals or as members of a social group – to reflect rationally upon their own action and to use precisely these reflections as a basis for practical change. The outstanding philosophical problem this creates for critical theory is to articulate a form of science in which the practical role of critical self-reflection and conscious human agency could be properly acknowledged and for which the rational empowerment of individuals could be a central aim. It is the need to resolve this problem that is at the heart of Jurgen Habermas's attempt to defend the idea of a critical social science – a science which, by acknowledging the ordinary individual's capacity for self-reflective judgement, is explicitly committed to sustaining and cultivating the role of human reason in social life. It is to Habermas's idea of a critical social science that I now turn.

III

For Habermas, as for many other contemporary philosophers, one of the most disturbing features of contemporary culture is the threat it poses for the future of human reason.[18] Modern societies, argues Habermas, have created conditions under which the Enlightenment concept of the rationally autonomous subject can no longer find adequate practical expression. Deprived of any significant role in the formulation of human purposes or social ends, reason has become an instrument for the effective pursuit of pre-established goals. Reduced to this kind of instrumental rationality, human reason has lost its critical thrust, judgement and deliberation have been replaced by calculation and technique, and reflective thought has been supplanted by a rigid conformity to methodical rules. Ours is a culture which, to use C. Wright Mills's felicitous phrase, is dominated by 'rationality without reason'.[19]

The mutilation inflicted on the Enlightenment concept of reason is seen by Habermas as an inevitable consequence of the successes and accomplishments of the natural sciences. This success has fuelled the belief that the scientific patterns of reasoning which have enabled us to extend our control over the world of nature can be used with equal success to extend our control over the human and social world as well. As a result, scientific rationality now operates as an uncritically accepted way of thinking that not only pervades modern intellectual disciplines – such as politics, history and economics – but also penetrates all aspects of everyday social life. Indeed, Habermas argues that the spread of scientific rationality has been so powerful that our understanding of the relationship between philosophy and science has become seriously distorted. Instead of accepting that science has to justify its knowledge claims against epistemological standards derived from philosophy, it is now assumed that epistemology has to be judged against standards laid down by science. Habermas calls this reduction of epistemology to the philosophy of science 'scientism', and he identifies it as 'the most influential philosophy of our time'. 'Scientism', he says, 'means science's belief in itself: that is, the conviction that we can no longer understand science as *one* form of possible knowledge, but rather must identify knowledge *with* science.'[20]

For Habermas, one of the adverse effects of 'scientism' has been to produce an impoverished understanding of the nature and role of the human and social sciences. Under the impact of scientistic assumptions, social theorizing has been transformed from an open-ended dialogue about the nature and conduct of social life into a value-free science requiring methodological sophistication and technical expertise. Because of this, ordinary individuals' confidence in their ability to determine the purposes and ends of their own actions has been eroded and they are now confronted by an image of the social world as an objective reality over which they themselves have no real control. In these circumstances the fundamental task of modern philosophy is to refute the epistemological assumptions on which this view of social science has been erected and to develop a philosophical justification for a form of social science which can rehabilitate the role of human reason in social affairs.

In *Knowledge and Human Interests*, Habermas pursues this task by mounting a philosophical critique designed to undermine the dominant scientistic epistemology in two specific ways. First, by showing that the natural sciences offer just one kind of knowledge among others, he refutes the claim that these sciences can define the epistemological standards by which all knowledge claims are to be assessed. Second, by outlining and defending a more comprehensive epistemology, he demonstrates that there are various legitimate forms of scientific inquiry, each with its own internal epistemological standards and each oriented towards the satisfaction of different human interests and needs.

Habermas contends that there are three such 'knowledge constitutive interests', each giving rise to a different form of 'science'. The first of these – the technical interest – is an interest in achieving mastery and control over the world of nature and it is constitutive of those 'empirical-analytic' sciences which seek to formulate explanatory and predictive knowledge about the natural world. But, as well as being 'interested' inhabitants of a world of nature, human beings also inhabit a social world. They thus have a 'practical' interest in understanding and participating in the cultural traditions which shape social life. This 'practical' interest gives rise to those 'historical-hermeneutic' sciences which produce interpretive knowledge of social life and thus make it more intelligible.

The third human interest – that of emancipation – derives from a fundamental desire to be free of those constraints on human reason – constraints of authority, ignorance, custom, tradition and the like – which impede the freedom of individuals to determine their purposes and actions on the basis of their own rational reflections. This 'emancipatory' interest thus gives rise to the idea of 'a critical social science': a science that aims to enlighten individuals about the origins of their existing purposes, beliefs and actions by promoting emancipatory knowledge – a form of reflective acquired self-knowledge which, by making individuals more consciously aware of the social and ideological roots of their self-understanding, thereby empowers them to think and act in a more rationally autonomous way.

The aims and values of a critical social science, as defined by Habermas, are, then, virtually identical to the aims and values of education as defined by Richard Peters. Both critical social science and education are expressions of an Enlightenment belief in the power of human reason. And both are predicated on the Enlightenment assumption that, through rational self-reflection, individuals can free themselves from the dictates of habit, prejudice and superstition and so become rationally autonomous agents. Given this similarity of aims and values, it should come as no surprise to find that Habermas's philosophical justification for a critical social science and Peters's philosophical justification for education proceed along similar lines. Both Habermas and Peters start from the premise that practical reason cannot be characterized simply as an instrument employed in the pursuit of pre-established goals. And both seek to vindicate the value and validity of practical reason by making use of 'transcendental' arguments about the *a priori* presuppositions inherent in the use of language.

Put briefly, Peters argues that what is distinctive of human beings is that their possession of language enables them to appraise the rational status of their own and other people's actions and beliefs. However, when individuals use language in this way – when, that is, they engage in rational discourse – they thereby give their assent to those intellectual norms in terms of which the rationality of any beliefs and actions can be judged.[21] Thus in the very act of asking and answering questions about what we should or should not do, we implicitly commit ourselves to those rational virtues – such as consistency, impartiality, clarity, precision, accuracy and respect for the facts – that are 'conceptually related to the pursuit of truth' and 'constitutive of the rational life'. But, as Peters also notes, 'reason cannot develop in a social vacuum'[22] and can be exercised only with a form of life governed by those social principles that the use of reason presupposes. For Peters, these are the principles of freedom, tolerance, equality and respect for persons, which are together constitutive of the democratic way of life. Thus, for Peters, 'Democracy is the articulation of reason in its social form.' 'A democratic society', he says, 'is one which upholds the use of reason in social life and personal autonomy as an educational aim'.[23]

Just as Peters defends the educational aim of rational autonomy by appealing to the presuppositions of ordinary practical discourse, so Habermas defends the idea of a critical social science by showing how it aims to create the conditions under which ideals implicit in everyday human language can be realized. Like Peters, Habermas erects his argument on an analysis of the concept of 'discourse'. To engage in 'discourse', he argues, requires that speakers are able to resolve disagreements through a critical dialogue in which the preconceptions, assumptions and beliefs of participants can be subject to rational argument.

> Discourse helps test the truth claims of opinions which the speakers no longer take for granted. In discourse the force of the better argument is the only permissible compulsion whereas co-operative search for the truth is the only permissible motive . . . Discourse produces nothing but argument.[24]

But such discourse, Habermas notes, can only proceed if participants are satisfied that certain claims about the validity of what is being said are being met. These 'validity claims' – that what is being said is comprehensible, that any factual assertions being made are true, that what is being said is, in the context, appropriate and justified, and that a speaker is being sincere and not trying to deceive the listener – are thus built into the very structure of discursive language. Hence, the very act of engaging in discourse presupposes a 'communicative rationality' such that any agreement reached through a discussion in which these four validity claims are met constitutes what Habermas calls a 'rational consensus' – an agreement arising precisely because 'the force of the better argument' has been allowed to prevail.

Habermas recognizes, of course, that this kind of purely rational discourse does not describe the way in which disagreements are actually resolved. It nevertheless creates the image of what Habermas calls an 'ideal speech situation' – a social context in which constraints on free and open dialogue have been excluded and in which impediments to rational argumentation and deliberation have been removed. Thus, by their very use of language, individuals reveal an unavoidable allegiance to those democratic forms of social life in which human reason has been 'emancipated' from the corrupting influence of tradition and ideology – precisely the form of social life which a critical social science seeks to create.

By grounding the case for a critical social science in the standards of rationality implicit in ordinary practical discourse, Habermas helps to liberate the social sciences from the confines of modern empiricist philosophy, and shows how they may be relocated in the mainstream of the Enlightenment philosophical tradition, with its defence of rational autonomy and of the potential of individuals to determine their actions on the basis of their own rational reflections. But, by doing this, Habermas had also provided the epistemological resources for developing an educational science which would be 'educational' precisely because it incorporates a commitment to the Enlightenment view of education which Peters's philosophy vindicates and supports. In this way, Habermas's justification for a critical social science is also a justification for an educational science that is no longer an 'empirical-analytic' science pursuing a technical interest in prediction and control, but a 'critical' science pursuing an educational interest in the development of rational autonomy and democratic forms of social life. It thus enables us to envisage the emergence of a science simultaneously 'critical', 'educational' and 'scientific'. It is 'critical' in that it provides standards for exposing and eliminating the inadequacies in existing modes of self-understanding and forms of social life. It is 'educational' in that it is itself an educative process designed to cultivate those qualities of mind that foster the development of rational individuals and the growth of democratic societies. And it is 'scientific' in that it generates reflective self-knowledge and defends the criteria on which the epistemological status of this knowledge depends. So understood, a critical educational science would not be a science *about* education but a science *for* education. Understood in this way, the aims of education and the aims of educational science would be one.

IV

Up to this point my main purpose has been to clarify and defend a particular idea of an educational science rather than to examine the details of its execution. In this final section I intend to provide a brief description of some of the main features of a critical educational science by pointing to some of the obvious ways in which it would differ from its traditional empiricist counterpart.

A critical educational science would be distinguishable from an empiricist educational science by virtue of its overall purpose, the kind of knowledge it produces and the method it employs. The purpose of an empiricist educational science is to improve the rationality of education through the practical application of knowledge it has itself produced. The purpose of a critical educational science would be to improve the rationality of education by enabling educational practitioners to refine the rationality of their practice for themselves. Thus, a critical educational science would not produce theoretical knowledge about educational practice, but the kind of educative self-knowledge that would reveal to practitioners the unquestioned beliefs and unstated assumptions in terms of which their practice was sustained. While an empiricist educational science seeks to replace the practical common-sense knowledge of practitioners with the theoretical 'objective' knowledge of science, a critical educational science seeks to encourage practitioners to treat their practical common-sense knowledge as a subject of critical reappraisal.

A critical educational science would not, therefore, evaluate the rationality of educational practice by employing the methods of the empirical sciences. It would instead employ the method of critique – a method which focuses on existing practice and which allows allegiance to be given only to those practices which can withstand critical confrontation with some shared understanding of education. From this perspective, education would not be interpreted as a natural phenomena but as a historically located and culturally embedded social practice which is vulnerable to ideological distortion, institutional pressures and other forms of non-educational constraint. Critique is thus a method for evaluating the rationality of practice from a cogent and clearly articulated educational point of view. It offers a method of self-evaluation which enables practitioners to reconstruct their practice as an *educational* practice in a rational and reflective way.

The kind of reasoning appropriate to the method of critique would not, of course, be that kind of technical reasoning which produces neutral knowledge about how to achieve some given end. It would instead be that form of ethically informed dialectical reasoning which generates practical knowledge about what ought to be done in a specific practical situation. It is 'ethically informed' reasoning because it aims to bring general educational values to bear on particular practical problems and concerns. And it is 'dialectical' because these general educational values are themselves clarified and developed in the light of the particular practical contexts in which they are being applied. The form of reasoning employed in a critical educational science is thus the kind of practical reasoning which Aristotle called *phronesis* – a form of reasoning in which educational values and educational practice would each be transformed by the other.

An empirical educational science can also be contrasted with a critical educational science in terms of the kind of theoretical community it sustains. Within an empiricist educational science, the theoretical community comprises an elite group of specialists who by virtue of their academic qualifications are deemed to possess the necessary professional expertise. A critical educational science, however, would create theoretical communities of educational practitioners committed to the rational development of their values and practices through a public process of discussion, argument and critique. As such, it would be a democratic, rather than an elitist, community committed to the formation and development of common educational purposes through critical reflection on existing policies and practice. It would thus be a community in which all participants were treated equally, in which there were no barriers to free and open communication and in which it was recognized that rationality, far from being the preserve of a scientific elite, is no one's property.

So understood, an educational science would be a moral science embedded in the rational values and democratic principles which education itself seeks to foster and promote. The practical realization of this idea of an educational science is not an easy task, for ours is a culture that considers education primarily in instrumental terms and interprets democracy as a system of political management rather than as a distinctive form of social and moral life. In such a culture, educational science is inevitably portrayed as a quasi-technical expertise in which non-technical, non-expert questions about the moral and social purposes of education are virtually ignored. It is thus scarcely surprising that the idea of an educational science as a form of democratic moral discourse now lacks the social context necessary for its practical application. Only a culture that is genuinely committed to educational aims conducive to the development of a more democratic society could allow such an educational science to become a practical possibility. Indeed, the kind of educational science I have described is nothing other than an elaboration of the democratic form of social and moral life of which it would itself be an integral part.

9 EPILOGUE:

CONFRONTING THE

POSTMODERNIST

CHALLENGE

It is no longer possible to hold the simple faith of the
Enlightenment that assured advance of science will produce
free institutions by dispelling ignorance and superstition –
the sources of human servitude and the pillars of oppressive
government.[1]

I

The unity of this book resides in its aspiration to link philosophical analysis to
educational commitment: to show how the intellectual basis of educational
inquiry requires educational theorists and researchers to formulate and conduct their activities around educational values and ideals. Against those who
still believe that 'disinterested' or 'objective' forms of theorizing and research
can be enlisted in the aid of educational values I have argued that their intellectual failure, together with their ideological complacency, will inevitably
lead to their terminal decline. Against those who argue that contemporary
society excludes the conditions required for the practical expression of the
forms of theorizing and research I have advocated, I have asserted that this is
not so much a refutation to my argument as a reflection of the uncritical way
in which the inherited ideology of contemporary society is now accepted and
understood. What I have also suggested is that the development of a more
adequate and less impoverished understanding of the moral, political and
intellectual promise of educational theory and research depends to some

considerable degree on relating educational inquiry to the outcomes of inquiries in the philosophy of science and the philosophy of the social sciences. This has been my task and nobody is more acutely conscious than me of the need for it to be performed in a more adequate and effective way.

One of the most pressing prerequisites to the future accomplishment of this task is to confront those who now insist on putting both the possibility and the desirability of its completion to the question. The project I have set for myself in this book – with its unqualified allegiance to emancipatory educational values – is essentially an Enlightenment project, reflecting a faith in the concept of 'modernity' to which the Enlightenment gave birth. With the rise of postmodernism, 'modernity' has now itself become the focus of critical attention and, as a result, commitment to the Enlightenment's emancipatory educational values is being dissipated. One response to the postmodernist threat – as exemplified by Habermas – is to argue that 'we must hold fast to the intentions of the Enlightenment . . . or give up the project of modernity as lost'.[2] But does postmodernism imply that the fate of the kind of educational inquiry proposed in this book depends on a simple choice between *either* reaffirming our faith in the Enlightenment tradition *or* abandoning its values and ideals? The purpose of this final chapter is to try to formulate a coherent response to the postmodernist challenge by situating the book's central argument more self-consciously within the Enlightenment tradition by which it is inspired and from which it is drawn.

II

One of the principle architects and chief exponents of the Enlightenment tradition was, of course, Immanuel Kant. Kant's central intellectual project was to provide the philosophical foundations for universal principles of rational justification that are independent of particular historical, social or cultural circumstances and that exhibit the capacity of all human beings for rational objectivity and truth. Kant believed that once the actions of individuals and societies were founded on such principles, reason would displace authority, the old social order would be demolished and a more rational, just and humane society would evolve. Thus the basic metaphor of the Enlightenment – that of 'light' – was intended to convey the message that the progressive development of human reason will illuminate the darkness of ignorance and superstition created by the religious and political institutions of the old despotic social order. Once freed from the restraints of prejudice dogma and tradition, humanity would have finally completed its long period of immaturity and individuals could become the autonomous subjects of their own development. Human reason would then become an objective historical force guiding the conduct and organization of social life and making the world a better place.

The practical task of the Enlightenment project was thus, in key part, an educational task: to develop in all people the universal power of reason and thereby to empower them to create collectively a form of social life that would satisfy their aspirations and needs. It is therefore unsurprising that Kant's dictum that the development of human reason enables people 'to escape from their self-incurred tutelage'[3] has become a pivotal feature of post-Enlightenment educational thought. Nor is it surprising that much of our strategic thinking about the role of education in modern democratic societies has been stimulated by – and has itself sought to promote – the Enlightenment's emancipatory ideals. If, as Anthony Giddens has claimed, 'emancipatory politics . . . reflects the characteristic orientation of modernity'[4] then it is only to be expected that modern educational thought will be underpinned by a belief in the possibility of an improvement of the human condition through the process of human emancipation.

The mobilizing principle behind most versions of emancipatory education is a commitment to educational aims and values associated with the Kantian notion of rational autonomy – aims and values which, historically, have been articulated in a variety of different ways but which always reflect the view that, through education, individuals may become rationally empowered to transform themselves and the social world in which they live. Of course, those subscribing to this view recognized that the educational aim of autonomy can only be realistically enacted in a society which has itself institutionalized the principles of rational justification. For Kant, as for other Enlightenment thinkers, a society which lacks objective standards of rational justification is a society in which the emancipatory aims of rational autonomy cannot be pursued. Thus a further feature of emancipatory educational ideas is that they invariably seek to promote the development of a democratic society – a society that is governed by rational principles and that promotes the freedom of all individuals to exercise their powers of rational thought.

Until as recently as the 1960s this Enlightenment vision of democratic societies peopled by rational autonomous individuals continued to underwrite the self-understandings in terms of which many educational theorists and researchers made sense of their intellectual ambitions and legitimized their political and cultural role. Today, however, this vision has been overtaken by a pervasive sense of limitation and a growing sense of inadequacy and failure. As a result, it is now far from evident that emancipatory theories do, or even could, exert any influence on the ways in which educational policy-makers and practitioners think and act. Indeed, one of the sure signs of the 1990s is the way in which emancipatory theories are now dismissed as utopian pie in the sky that fly in the face of ordinary common sense and the plain facts of everyday life. In many ways, we now seem to be witnessing a reactionary drive to jettison the last vestiges of enlightened educational theorizing under the banner of a neo-pragmatic, anti-intellectual educational ideology that has raised common-sense beliefs to the status of self-authorizing truth.

But perhaps the most depressing aspect of these recent developments is the way in which this wholesale abdication of Enlightenment educational values has been raised to a high point of theoretical sophistication under the name of 'postmodernism'. Whatever else it means, 'postmodernism' is intended to announce that 'modernity' – the 'age of reason' to which the Enlightenment gave birth – has now given way to a 'postmodern condition' which has produced irreversible changes to the way in which we experience and relate to modern ideas and modern forms of life. In this new cultural configuration, educational theorizing and research that seek to give expression to the enlightenment ideas of emancipation, empowerment and rational autonomy lack both analytic credibility and political legitimacy. Indeed, what, more than anything else, characterizes the postmodern world is 'a common rhetoric of rebellion against the Enlightenment narrative'[5] – a realization that forms of theorizing and research that derive from the Enlightenment are no longer adequate when we try to make sense of our contemporary social and cultural world.

III

What is to be our response to the postmodern challenge? One response is to assert that its obituaries to modernity are premature, that there is no need to abandon our emancipatory educational theories and that our existing strategies for achieving Enlightenment educational goals remain valid. Another response is to retreat to a postmodernist stance that abandons all enlightened educational thinking and regards any suggestion that human reason may be an indispensable aid to human emancipation as obsolete. The problem with the first of these responses is that, by pretending that nothing of importance has happened, its advocates are forced to defend old orthodoxes that postmodernism now at best castigates as ethnocentric and at worst ridicules as absurd and naive. The problem with the second response is that it seems to suggest that those who are influenced by, and perhaps sympathetic to, postmodernism should not only disengage from emancipatory educational values, but retreat to a sceptical stance of indifference from which it is impossible to endorse any principled view of education at all.[6]

Formulating an educational response to postmodernism is further complicated by the fact that, true to its own 'celebration of diversity', there are a number of different 'postmodernisms', each theorizing the meaning of postmodernity in a different way. Those who believe that we are now experiencing a complete rupture from modernity use the term 'postmodernity' to identify an entirely new cultural configuration that has its own distinctive and unique features.[7] But for those who recognize the continuities as well as the discontinuities between modern and postmodern times, postmodernity indicates not so much that modernity has come to an end as that it has now entered a new phase.[8] Similarly, although postmodern theorists all agree that the contemporary era is sufficiently different to warrant being described as a 'postmodern condition', questions about the causes, nature and significance of this 'condition' remain a matter for disagreement and dispute. As a result there are now numerous 'postmodernisms' that vary not just in their verdicts on the meaning of 'postmodernity', but also in their assessments of the kind of theoretical, political and educational response that it requires.

It is no doubt the vagueness and ambiguities surrounding the concept of postmodernity that have given plausibility to the view that its real importance is not so much that it identifies a new social reality, but that it makes explicit a new attitude towards social reality – a way of relating to modern conditions that transcends the bounds of modernist thinking itself.[9] So understood, the concept of 'postmodernity' is an expression of the growing realization that it is no longer possible to regard the truth of the Enlightenment narrative as self-evident or to believe that the realization of its emancipatory vision is simply a matter of time. It is this gradual erosion of the self-confidence and self-understanding of those who have embraced Enlightenment ideals that, according to Bauman, the vague notion of 'postmodernity' so effectively captures and describes.

> If the concept of 'postmodernity' has no other value, it has at least this one: it supplies a new and external vantage point from which some aspects of that world that came into being in the aftermath of the Enlightenment . . . (aspects not visible, or allocated secondary importance when observed from inside the unfinished process) acquire saliency and can be turned into pivotal issues of the discourse.[10]

Interpreted in this way, postmodernity does not refer to the 'end of modernity'. Instead, it describes a new self-understanding which, by making modernity itself an object for critical reflection, makes its Enlightenment assumptions more transparent and thus more open to question and doubt. But if postmodernity is 'no more than the modern mind taking a long attentive look at itself, at its condition and its past work',[11] then the educational significance of postmodernity is not to imply that our emancipatory vision of education is no longer viable or worth promoting. Rather, it is that it challenges us to defend our confidence in this vision from an intellectual perspective in which the prospects and desirability of the future fulfilment of the Enlightenment project can no longer be anticipated or assumed. In short, the real challenge of postmodernism is that it forces us to reconsider our commitment to emancipatory education in a way which does not simply dismiss the central insights of postmodernist thought.

In philosophy, postmodernism can be construed in a broad sense to include a number of theoretical positions that collectively seek to move beyond the Enlightenment conceptions of reason and the rationally autonomous subject which received their clearest expression in the philosophy of Kant. For present purposes, the postmodern insights that most seriously challenge our emancipatory view of educational inquiry are those stemming from its critique of Kant's 'foundationalist' philosophy – a philosophy designed to show that the Enlightenment concept of the rationally autonomous subject did not simply apply to a particular culture or society but was grounded in *a priori* truths about the 'universal essence' of human nature itself. At the risk of oversimplification, three of the familiar postmodernist strategies used to undermine and discredit this foundationalist logic can be rapidly stated. The first is to call into question the Enlightenment's universal, *a priori* and absolutist conception of reason. To its universality, postmodernists counterpose the 'local' determinants of what counts as rational thought and action; to its *a priori* necessity, they counterpose its fallibility and its contingency; and to its absolutism they insist that rationality is always relative to time and place.

What, second, postmodernism opposes and denies is the Enlightenment idea of a disembodied 'rational autonomous subject'. In opposition to the assumption that the self has at its centre an essential human nature that predates history and is prior to a particular form of social life, postmodernism counterposes an image of the self as 'decentred': a centreless configuration mediated and constituted through the discourses learned and acquired in becoming a participant in a historical culture. Since there is no way to step outside such discourses, since our sense of who and what we are is always shaped by the discourses circulating in our historical context, there is no essential 'self' to discover. In Heidegger's phrase, 'Language speaks man.'

Third, and closely interwoven with the postmodernist critique of Enlightenment conceptions of reason and the autonomous subject, is its critique of the Enlightenment distinction between the 'knowing subject' and an 'objective' world to be known. Against this, postmodernism insists that the subject's knowledge of the world is always pre-interpreted: it is always situated in a conceptual scheme, part of a text, internal to a tradition outside of which there are only other conceptual schemes, texts and traditions and beyond which it is impossible to stand. It follows from this that knowledge is never 'disinterested' or 'objective' and that the Enlightenment idea of the knowing subject disengaged from the world is a myth. It also follows that the Enlightenment assumption that philosophy can provide the epistemological 'foundations' on which scientific disciplines can be erected and their theories can be objectively justified is false. What postmodernism insists is that there is no realm of 'objective' truths to which science has exclusive access, no privileged position that enables philosophers to transcend the particularities of their own culture and traditions, no Archimedian point which can provide philosophical inquiry with a neutral ahistorical starting point. In Richard Rorty's words, such a view of philosophy is simply a futile attempt 'to step outside our skins and compare ourselves with something absolute . . . to escape from the finitude of one's time and place, the "merely conventional" and contingent aspects of one's life.'[12]

Clearly, many of these postmodernist ideas are closely related to the contemporary intellectual debates with which this book has been concerned. For example, the attempt (in Chapter 4) to reconstruct the notion of educational practice by rehabilitating the Aristotelian concept of *praxis* explicitly incorporates the postmodernist rejection of the Enlightenment distinction between reason and tradition. Similarly, the analysis of the scientific status of educational research (in Chapters 5 and 6) draws on a post-empiricist philosophy of science which resonates closely with the postmodernist critique of the Enlightenment concept of rationality. Indeed, it would be no exaggeration to say that one way of reading this book is as a sustained effort to reject and replace the rationalistic view of 'objective' educational inquiry that the Kantian notion of practical reason has bequeathed.

But to accept that postmodernism represents a significant turning point does not mean that the Enlightenment has outlived its usefulness or that forms of educational inquiry aimed at promoting its emancipatory vision have been built on a utopian dream. Nor does accepting the postmodernist critique of the epistemological foundations on which emancipatory educational values were first erected mean that these values cannot outlive the philosophical justification that the Enlightenment provided for them. It simply means that these values can no longer be characterized in terms of the Enlightenment philosophy that played such an important role in their initial formulation and that the concepts of reason and the human subject that first made the educational aims of emancipation and empowerment possible may now be preventing us from accepting that our 'modern' understanding of educational inquiry has to be changed.

Thus, the central challenge that postmodernism poses for the kind of educational inquiry proposed in this book can now be formulated in a more precise way. How can we restore our confidence in our emancipatory vision of education? Can we devise a way of thinking about educational inquiry which is 'modern' in the sense that it does not abandon emancipatory ideals but 'postmodern' in the sense that it abandons the foundationalist Enlightenment narrative within which these ideals have hitherto been articulated? Can we construct a strategy for guiding the future of educational inquiry which recognizes that the only way to preserve an emancipatory concept of education is critically to revise its meaning so as to take account of the postmodern condition in which we now live? What would a postmodern strategy for educational inquiry – a strategy that is seriously concerned to come to grips with the phenomena of postmodernity – look like?

In the first place, it would be a strategy that no longer pretends that the emancipatory values it sought to promote could be justified by an appeal to epistemological foundations. Instead, it would acknowledge that what justifies our continuing commitment to these values is the conviction that the problems of irrationality and injustice to which the Enlightenment was a response still exist. In other words, what justifies our continuing allegiance to these values is their congruence with our present understanding of ourselves and our particular historical situation and our realization that, given the educational traditions through which our dominant educational discourses and practices have been constructed, these still remain the most reasonable and appropriate educational values to adopt. Second, conscious of the need to give up the abstract Enlightenment idea of an ahistorical reason common to all people, such a strategy would not assume that its eventual success was guaranteed by some inexorable law of 'human nature'. Instead, it would be tempered by a realization that there are no universal standards of rationality external to history and tradition and that 'human nature' is itself socially constructed through an initiation into pre-existing discourses and practices.

Finally, recognizing that there was no 'objective' standpoint from which to endorse the superiority of the emancipatory values it sought to advance, such a strategy would not regard educational inquiry as the embodiment of universally valid educational aims but as a contingent human project which arose in certain historical circumstances and which now needs to be reinterpreted and revised to meet the new cultural conditions that the notion of 'postmodernity' articulates and describes. But in doing this it would not necessarily suppress the Enlightenment vocabulary of emancipation and empowerment or totally abandon its epistemological language of objectivity and truth. Instead it would interpret the language of the Enlightenment as directing us to nothing outside itself and hence to a more self-conscious realization that there is no transient knowledge to which educational inquiry can appeal which stands beyond or behind the discourse which the language of emancipatory education itself constructs.

Thus what would make educational theorizing and research 'postmodern' is not a willingness to relinquish a 'modern' commitment to emancipatory values but a willingness to relinquish the Enlightenment presumption that those values have to be erected on philosophical 'foundations'. 'Postmodern' educational inquiry would thus continue to encompass forms of critical educational inquiry aimed at a distinctly 'modern' task: to expose the tensions and contradictions between emancipatory educational values and prevailing educational policies and practices in order to indicate how contemporary educational institutions may be reconstructed so that they are able to operate in a more emancipatory way. But this type of educational inquiry would no longer try to offer any philosophical guarantees for the kinds of theorizing and research it advocated and it would openly acknowledge that there was no ahistorical standpoint from which to endorse the emancipatory values it sought to advance. By conceding that there is nothing external to experience, no 'essence' to human nature, no 'destiny' towards which history inevitably moves, it would also concede that the only way to justify itself was by appealing to its faith in the willingness of ordinary educational practitioners to reconstruct their practice in ways which would give expression to emancipatory educational values and ideals.

Thus it turns out that this book may be read as both a 'modern' and a 'postmodern' text: 'modern' in the sense that it advocates a form of educational inquiry that speaks to the Enlightenment vision of emancipatory education but 'postmodern' because it advocates educational inquiries which allow this vision to be pursued on the basis of the contingent experienced-based knowledge of ordinary educational practitioners rather than by resorting to objective knowledge drawn from some external authoritative source. It thus anticipates the future emergence of a 'dephilosophized' or 'post-philosophical' strategy for educational inquiry which will be premised on very different assumptions from those that the Enlightenment supplied: the open-ended formation of the human subject; the futility of utopian ideas about a ready-made fixed self; the realization that there is no corpus of 'objective' knowledge that stands outside the historical context which endows it with meaning and significance. In formulating such a strategy old certainties will have to be abandoned and new questions will have to be asked. What follows, in educational terms, from a realization that the Enlightenment tradition is open and indeterminate and hence subject to reinterpretation and reconstruction as it passes from one historical context to another? Does educational theory best defend Enlightenment ideals by seeking to multiply and extend emancipatory educational practices rather than by providing them with rational foundations? What are the implications of conceding that the notion of the rational autonomous individual has now become a hindrance to the future development of educational theory and research?

All too frequently, postmodernism is taken to imply that we should disengage from those questions, deconstruct our emancipatory values and dismiss the Enlightenment vision of education as a utopian dream. If educational theorists and researchers succumb to this attitude, educational inquiry will quickly lose its critical thrust and degenerate into little more than a source of theoretical legitimation for the *status quo*. What I have tried to suggest is that the only way to ensure that this does not happen is to develop a post-postmodernist educational strategy that will enable educational theorists and researchers to re-engage with – rather than disengage from – the Enlightenment educational tradition and to reconstruct – rather than deconstruct – their emancipatory educational values and ideals. Educational theorists and researchers do not yet know how to develop such a strategy and understanding how to do so is an indispensable precondition to further advancing the kind of educational inquiry advocated in this book. But it is only by virtue of such an understanding that we will better be able to appreciate why postmodernism should be regarded not as a threat to critical educational inquiry but as an indispensable aid to the future accomplishment of its goals.

NOTES

Prologue: Theorizing educational practices
(Stephen Kemmis)

1 On the distinction between social order and social movement, see Touraine (1981).
2 Compare Ludwig Wittgenstein's (1963: 103) image of the 'conjuring trick' of behaviourism: 'How does the philosophical problem about mental processes and states and about behaviourism arise? – The first step is the one that altogether escapes our notice. We talk of processes and states and leave their nature undecided. Some time perhaps we shall know more about them – we think. But that is just what commits us to a particular way of looking at the matter. For we have a definite concept of what it means to know a process better. (The decisive move in the conjuring trick has been made, and it was the very one we thought quite innocent.) – And now the analogy which was to make us understand our thoughts falls to pieces. So we have to deny the yet uncomprehended process in the yet undeveloped medium. And now it looks as if we had denied mental processes. And naturally we don't want to deny them.'
3 Foucault (1970).
4 Weber (1964: 88).
5 Eco (1984).
6 Hidness (1977: 8).
7 See, for example, Smith et al. (1950), Stanley et al. (1956) and Connell et al. (1962).
8 See, for example, O'Connor (1957) and Hirst (1966). For a retrospective review of the educational theory movement by some of its central figures, see the chapters by Hirst and R. S. Peters in Hirst, P. H. (1983).
9 Schwab (1969).
10 Schwab (1974).
11 McKeon (1952).
12 Aristotle (1955).

13 On practical reasoning, see Gauthier (1963); for a good account of practical reasoning in curriculum, see Reid (1978). For a recent analysis of different varieties of practical reasoning in the philosophy of justice, see MacIntyre (1988).

14 Habermas, J. (1972, 1974).

15 For a history of the Frankfurt School, see Jay (1973). A major synthesizing work outlining the critical theory perspective of the Frankfurt School (written by one of its directors) is Horkheimer, M. (1972). *Critical Theory*. New York, Seabury Press.

16 The theory of communicative competence has developed and evolved through most of Habermas's recent work (e.g. 1970b, 1979, 1984, 1987).

17 Schon (1983). Concerning reflection among learners (especially adult learners and tertiary students), rather than teachers, see Bould *et al.* (1985).

18 Schon (1983).

19 For a critique of the 'rationalistic theory of action' underpinning much recent social theory, see Hindess (1977).

20 An example of an exception to this generalization is Hamilton (1977). A well-known example from sociology is Geer (1964).

21 Carr and Kemmis (1986).

22 Critical reflection does not only involve considering the adequacy of our practices in the light of our theories, it also involves considering the adequacy of theories in the light of our practices. On the one side, critical examination might involve considering the adequacy of our practices in the light of our theories, for example in relation to such matters as (a) the extent to which our practices realize the intentions of our theories, (b) the extent to which our practices embody the values and traditions which give them meaning and significance (given the exigencies of existing personal, institutional and historical circumstances) and/or (c) the extent to which our practices create new possibilities for theorizing (describing, understanding, explaining, justifying) the social, political and educational processes of which we are part. On the other side, it might also include considering such matters as (a) the extent to which the terms of our theories accurately, consistently and comprehensively describe our practices, (b) the extent to which our interpretations of the meaning and signficance of our practices accord with the evidence of (our own and others') observations of their nature, purposes, circumstances and consequences, and/or (c) the extent to which our explanations account for the accumulated evidence of observation and interpretation, providing us with new frameworks for action, and giving us a new sense of how we can act in terms of the tension between the actual and the possible. A thoroughly critical perspective on the relationship of theory and practice will of course involve alternating between these two perspectives – treating both theory and practice as problematic, each in relation to the other.

23 Stenhouse (1979).

24 See MacIntyre (1981) on the distinctions between activities and practices (p.175) and between practices and institutions (p.181).

25 Compare MacIntyre (1988 12-13): 'A tradition is an argument extended through time in which certain fundamental agreements are defined and redefined in terms of two kinds of conflict: those with critics and enemies external to the tradition who reject all or at least key parts of those fundamental agreements, and those internal, interpretive debates through which the meaning and rationale of the fundamental agreements come to destroy the basis of common fundamental agreement, so that either a tradition divides into two or more warring components, whose adherents are transformed into external critics of each other's positions, or else the tradition loses all coherence and fails to survive. It can also happen that two traditions, hitherto independent and even antagonistic, can come to recognise certain possibilities of fundamental agreement and reconstitute themselves as a single, more complex

debate . . . To appeal to tradition is to insist that we cannot adequately identify either our own commitments or those of others in the argumentative conflicts of the present except by situating them within those histories which made them what they have now become.'

26 And one which MacIntyre is unlikely to accept, given his scathing passing comment on 'neo-Weberian organisation theorists and the heirs of the Frankfurt School' (of social science, among whom Habermas must undoubtedly be counted), who, says MacIntyre, 'unwittingly collaborate in the theatre of the present' by defining the self in terms of its relationship to bureaucracy, despite their criticisms of bureaucratic modes of organization and consciousness. See MacIntyre (1981: 29).

27 Habermas (1970b: 372).

28 McCarthy (1975: xvii).

Introduction: Becoming an educational philosopher

1 Hegel (1952: 11).
2 Burgess (1987).
3 Eagleton (1990: 34).
4 Peters (1966a: 15).
5 Bell (1962).
6 Hirst (1974: 1–2).
7 See, for example, Gellner (1959) and Mundle (1970).
8 Kuhn (1970).
9 See, for example, Peters (1977b).
10 MacIntyre (1984) and Taylor (1984b).

1   The gap between theory and practice

1 Inglis (1985: 40).
2 Numerous examples abound. See, for instance, Chapter 5 of O'Connor (1957), Hardie (1957), Hirst (1963) and Best (1965).
3 The clearest indication that this transformation was under way was the introduction of the *Students Library of Education* by Routledge and Kegan Paul in 1966. Of particular significance was the 'parent' volume: Tibble (1966). This contains not only the rationale for a 'disciplines' approach as such, but also an attempt by representatives of each of the educational disciplines to explain and justify the importance of their own particular contributions.
4 See, for example, how Peters (1973), one of the most active supporters of the disciplines approach, began to recognize some of its drawbacks.
5 See Adams (1928).
6 O'Connor (1957).
7 Hirst (1957).
8 Kuhn (1970).
9 See, for example, Filmer *et al.* (1972).
10 The idea that the social sciences have no useful contribution to make to the theoretical study of education is just as defective as the idea that they are, themselves, a species of 'educational theory'. For a rejection of any attempt to insulate educational theory from the insights of the social sciences, see Chapter 2.

2   Theories of theory and practice

1 Eagleton (1990: 26–7).

2 That this is a peculiarly modern view of how theoretical and practical matters are related is evident from the history of the subject. See Lobkowicz (1967).
3 For an extended discussion of the social nature of educational thought and practice see Langford (1985).
4 For a fuller discussion of this issue see Chapter 1.
5 A philosophical discussion of the role of 'common sense' in educational theory is to be found in Pring (1977). For a more recent attempt to link common sense and educational theory see Hirst (1983).
6 The standard rationale for the 'applied science' approach can be found in the opening chapters of most educational research textbooks. The clearest and most influential philosophical arguments in its favour remains O'Connor (1957).
7 The roots of the 'practical' approach are clearly Aristotelian. Its most eloquent modern advocate in the field of education is Schwab (1969). The role of 'practical' thinking in curriculum theory and research is explored by Reid (1978).
8 The philosophical basis of critical theory is invariably associated with the writings of Habermas (1972, 1974, 1979). However, its central insights are clearly evident in much of the literature of the philosophy of the social sciences. See, for example, MacIntyre (1971), Bernstein (1972) and Fay (1975). For an attempt to develop a critical approach to educational theory and research see Carr and Kemmis (1986). For a 'critical' analysis of the curriculum see Inglis (1985).
9 Habermas (1972).

3   Adopting an educational philosophy

1 Gramsci (1971).
2 Popper (1972).
3 Illich (1971).

4   What is an educational practice?

1 MacIntyre (1981: 180).
2 As far as I can tell, there are no publications in the philosophy of education explicitly concerned with the concept of an educational practice. What are available in the general philosophical literature, and what have influenced the argument of this paper more than anything else are the various discussions of 'practice' in the work of Hans-George Gadamer. See, in particular, Gadamer (1967, 1980b, 1981).
3 Gauthier (1963).
4 This is a strategy employed by Paul Hirst as part of his analysis of educational theory. See Hirst (1983a).
5 Ryle (1949: Chapter 2).
6 *Ibid*: 29.
7 *Ibid*: 26.
8 *Ibid*.
9 *Ibid*: 41.
10 Several critical studies have made this point. See, for example, Martin (1961).
11 See, in particular, Peters (1959).
12 This is, of course, a Wittgensteinian insight which was developed with some skill by Peter Winch (1958).
13 The relationship between conceptual change and social change is discussed in some detail in Skinner (1980).
14 This view of the relationship between philosophy and social change is, of course, Hegelian. For a fuller account see Taylor (1984a).

15 The history of the concept of practice is covered in some detail in Lobkowicz (1967).
16 Historical explanations of how and why this became a problem are offered in Lobkowicz (1977).
17 What Gadamer refers to as 'pre-judgement', 'for-conceptions' and 'prejudice'. See Gadamer (1980a).
18 The epistemological role of the notion of tradition has been stressed by a diverse range of philosophers. See, for example, Oakeshott (1966), MacIntyre (1981) and Bernstein (1983).
19 Gadamer (1980a: 249) puts the point vividly: 'That which has been sanctioned by tradition has an authority that is nameless.'
20 Again, the point is eloquently put by Gadamer (1980a: 261): 'Tradition is not simply a precondition into which we come but we produce it ourselves, in so much as we understand, we participate in the evolution of tradition and hence further determine it ourselves'.
21 The claim that our own modern culture has discarded tradition for just these reasons is central to the argument of MacIntyre (1981).
22 See Gadamer (1980b) for both an account of Aristotle's notion of 'practical philosophy' and the case for its modern revival.
23 Aristotle's fullest account of deliberation and practical reasoning is to be found in Book IV, Chapter 9 of *The Nicomachean Ethics* (1955).
24 As Aristotle puts it: 'He who deliberates well, deliberates correctly' (*ibid*: 1142b).
25 For a detailed exposition of Aristotle's notion of judgement see Beiner (1983: Chapters 4 and 5).
26 See Ball (1977), Gadamer (1967, 1981) and MacIntyre (1981).
27 See, for example, Schwab (1969) and Van Manen (1977).

5 Can educational research be scientific?

1 John Dewey, quoted in Cronbach and Suppes (1969).
2 See, for example, the debate between Professors Hirst and O'Connor in Langford and O'Connor (1973).
3 Young (1971).
4 Dockrell and Hamilton (1980).
5 Freeman and Jones (1980).
6 See, for example, Cohen and Manion (1980) and Verma and Beard (1981).
7 The most influential of these remains Winch (1958). See also Outhwaite (1975).
8 Bantock (1965).
9 Ryan (1970) and Von Wright (1971).
10 Langford (1971).
11 Gauthier (1963).
12 Popper (1969) and Kekes (1977).
13 Popper (1960). *The Poverty of Historicism*. London, Routledge and Kegan Paul.
14 See, for example, Scheffler, I. (1967). *Science and Subjectivity*. New York, Bobbs-Merrill.
15 Thomas, D. (1979). *Naturalism and Social Science*. London, Cambridge University Press.
16 Lakatos, I. (1970). 'Falsification and the methodology of scientific research programmes', in I. Lakatos and A.E. Musgrove (eds.) *Criticism and the Growth of Knowledge*. London, Cambridge University Press.
17 Putman, H. (1981). *Reason Truth and History*. London, Cambridge University Press.

18 Brown, H.I. (1977). *Perception, Theory and Commitment: the new philosophy of science.* Chicago Ill., Chicago Precedent Publishing Co.
19 Pring, R. (1977). 'Common sense and education', *Proceedings of the Philosophy of Education Society of Great Britain*, 11, 57–77.

6 Philosophy, values and an educational science

1 Morris (1972: 60–1).
2 The historical question of why this urge to adopt a neutral stance took such a hold on educational research has already received some attention. See Hamilton (1980).
3 The various arguments used to support this view of the relationship between values and educational research can be found in Phillips (1971).
4 Searle (1972).
5 Habermas (1972).
6 Laslett and Runciman (1967).
7 Brown (1977).
8 Kuhn (1970).
9 Partridge (1968) and MacIntyre (1972).
10 Taylor (1967: 42).
11 *Ibid*: 56–7.
12 Fay (1975), Bernstein (1976), Thomas (1979) and Lloyd (1983).
13 Hardie (1942), O'Connor (1957), Peters (1966b) and Moore (1974).
14 Moore (1982: 22).
15 *Ibid*: 31–2.
16 *Ibid*: 32–3.
17 Hollis (1977) and Atkinson (1983).
18 Hollis (1977: 2–3).
19 For a detailed elaboration of the criticism see Carr (1979).
20 Dagenais (1972), Hollis (1977) and Thomas (1979).
21 Thomas (1979: 142).
22 Foot (1967), MacIntyre (1967), Winch (1971), Williams (1972) and Quinton (1975).
23 MacIntyre (1972: 266).
24 Williams (1972: 75).
25 This point has been emphasized by R.S. Peters. 'Philosophy of Education', he writes, 'is in need of a more explicit theory of human nature. In the past concepts . . . have been treated in too much of a vacuum . . . A more adequate theory must take more account of human nature as a whole' Peters (1983: 51).
26 For an early affirmation and detailed analysis of this point see Dunlop (1970).
27 In the case of Mannheim, this sort of analysis is undertaken in Thomas (1979: 152–6).
28 Habermas (1972).
29 The implications of Habermas's theory for educational research are far-reaching. For a discussion of these see Carr and Kemmis (1986: Chapters 5 and 6).
30 Fay (1975) and Bernstein (1976).
31 This point transcends the arguments about whether educational research should be 'scientific' and 'quantitative' or 'illuminative' and 'qualitative'. Proponents of both these views share the common assumptions that the educational researcher is 'disinterested' in educational values and goals.
32 Bantock (1965).
33 Travers (1969).
34 For a philosophical analysis of the scientific status of educational research see Chapter 5.

35 Hesse (1980: 171).

36 The most influential post-empiricist texts were Hanson (1958), Kuhn (1970), Lakatos (1970) and Feyerabend (1975).

37 Clear accounts of the central ideas and arguments of the post-empiricist philosophy of science can be found in Brown (1977) and Hesse (1980).

38 For a discussion on this point see Putnam (1981).

39 The implications of the under-determination thesis and of the need to appeal to non-empirical criteria of theory choice provided the starting point for Feyerabend's (1975) 'anarchistic' view of knowledge.

40 The argument for the theory-ladenness of observations was initially developed by Hanson (1958).

41 The notion of 'research programme' and the concepts of 'problem situation' and 'positive heuristic' are taken from Lakatos (1970).

42 The most forceful and influential statement of the metaphysical nature of science remains Kuhn (1970).

43 This problem has been explored in some detail in Scheffler (1967).

44 Hesse (1978: 2).

45 Fay (1975), Hesse (1980) and Thomas (1979).

46 Stenhouse (1975) and Elliott (1978a).

47 For a discussion of educational research as a form of 'moral science' see Elliott (1983).

7   Whatever happened to action research?

1 Kolakowski (1968).

2 Sanford (1970).

3 Lewin (1946, 1952).

4 Sanford (1970: 129).

5 *Ibid*: 127.

6 *Ibid*: 128–9.

7 Stenhouse (1975).

8 Elliott (1978b).

9 Prominent among these was the Classroom Action Research Network (CARN) based at the Cambridge Institute of Education.

10 One of the most successful of these was the Teacher Pupil Interaction and Quality of Learning Project (TIQL), funded by the Schools Council.

11 See, for example, Hopkins (1985) and Kemmis and McTaggart (1988).

12 A notable exception is John Elliott, who during the past decade has published a number of papers aimed at making theoretical sense of the notion of action research. For a recent example, see Elliott (1987).

13 Hustler *et al.* (1986: 207).

14 Winter (1987).

15 Winter (1989).

16 Winter (1987: 4).

17 *Ibid*: 150.

18 For a critical history of positivism, see Kolakowski (1972), Giddens (1974) and Bryant (1985).

19 The different purposes served by these two aspects of inquiry were well understood by the Greeks. As one modern political philosopher puts it: 'while *philosophia* tended to stress the arduous difficulty awaiting those who sought truth, the devotees of *methodus* began to emphasise the economy . . . of faithfully following a prescribed sequence of mental steps . . . of adhering to a beaten path' (Wolin 1972).

8 The idea of an educational science

1 Dewey quoted in Westbrook (1991: 502).
2 O'Connor (1973: 59).
3 *Ibid*: 48.
4 Hesse (1980: 171).
5 The central arguments of the post-empiricist philosophy of science can be found in Brown (1977).
6 See Capters 5 and 6.
7 In Warnock (1962: 185–6).
8 See Kant (1959).
9 Peters's most comprehensive statement of his educational philosophy remains *Ethics and Education* (1966a).
10 Peters writes: 'Man is a creature who lives under the demands of reason . . . Human life is only intelligible on the assumption that the demands of reason are admitted and woven into the fabric of human life'. (Peters 1977c: 254).
11 See particularly Peters (1977a, 1979).
12 'Rational autonomy', wrote Peters, 'has to be understood in contrast to unthinking conformity and rigid adherence to dogma . . . It requires a willingness to learn and to revise opinions and assumptions when confronted with situations that challenge them'. (Peters 1977a).
13 Peters (1979: 469).
14 See, for example, Mills (1959), Gouldner (1973), Gadamer (1980b), Hearn (1985) and Fay (1987).
15 Habermas (1972).
16 The standard text on the early history of critical theory remains Jay (1973).
17 The definitive statement of the important differences between these 'traditional' forms of social theory and 'critical' theory is in Horkheimer (1972).
18 See, for example, Habermas (1970a), Gadamer (1980b) and MacIntyre (1981).
19 Mills (1959: 159–60).
20 Habermas (1972: 4).
21 Peters (1966: Chapter 5; 1977a: Chapter 5).
22 Peters (1979: 469).
23 *Ibid*.
24 Habermas (1974: 168).

9 Epilogue: resisting the postmodernist challenge

1 Dewey (1939: 131).
2 Habermas (1987: 326–7).
3 Kant (1963: 9).
4 Giddens (1991: 211).
5 Mestrovic (1991). *The Coming Fin de Siecle*, quoted in Smart (1993: 28).
6 This problem is discussed at some length by the contributors to Squires (1993).
7 This view is taken by Frederick Jameson (1984).
8 This is the position taken by Stephen Toulmin (1990).
9 Something like this interpretation of the notion of 'postmodernity' is proposed by Smart (1993: Chapter 1).
10 Bauman (1992: 102–3).
11 Bauman (1991: 272).
12 Rorty (1982: 6).

REFERENCES AND
BIBLIOGRAPHY

Adams, J. (1928) *Educational Theories*. London: Ernest Benn.

Aristotle (1955) *The Nicomachean Ethics* (trans. J.A.K. Thomson). London: Penguin.

Atkinson, C. (1983) *Making Sense of Piaget: the Philosophical Roots*. London: Routledge and Kegan Paul.

Ball, T. (ed.) (1977) *Political Theory and Praxis: New Perspectives*. Minneapolis: University of Minnesota Press.

Bantock, G. (1965) 'Educational research: a criticism', in G. Bantock, *Education and Values: Essays in the Theory of Education*. London: Faber.

Bauman, Z. (1991) *Modernity and Ambivalence*. Cambridge: Polity Press.

Bauman, Z. (1992) *Intimations of Postmodernity*. London: Routledge.

Beiner, R. (1983) *Political Judgement*. London: Methuen.

Bell, D. (1962) *The End of Ideology: on the Exhaustion of Political Ideas in the Fifties*. London: Collier-Macmillan.

Bernstein, R.J. (1972) *Praxis and Action*. London: Duckworth.

Bernstein, R.J. (1976) *The Restructuring of Social and Political Theory*. Oxford: Basil Blackwell.

Bernstein, R.J. (1983) *Beyond Objectivism and Subjectivism: Science, Hermeneutics and Praxis*. Oxford: Blackwell.

Best, E. (1965) 'Common confusions in educational theory', in R.D. Archambault (ed.) *Philosophical Analysis and Education*. London: Routledge and Kegan Paul.

Bould, D., Keogh, R. and Walker, D. (1985) *Reflection: Turning Experience into Learning*. London: Kogan Page.

Brown, H.I. (1977) *Perception, Theory and Commitment: the New Philosophy of Science*. Chicago, IL: Precedent Publishing Co.

Bryant, C.G.A. (1985) *Positivism in Social Theory and Research*. Basingstoke: Macmillan.

Burgess, A. (1987) *Little Wilson and Big God*. London: Heinemann.

Carr, W. (1979) 'Philosophical styles and educational theory', *Educational Studies*, **5**, 1.

Carr, W. and Kemmis, S. (1986) *Becoming Critical: Education, Knowledge and Action Research*. Brighton: Falmer Press.

Cohen, L. and Manion, L. (1980) *Research Methods in Education*. London: Croom Helm.

Connell, W.F. *et. al.* (1962) *The Foundations of Education*. Sydney: Novak.

Cronbach, L.J. and Suppes, P. (1969) *Research for Tomorrow's Schools*. Lodon: Macmillan.

Dagenais, J.J. (1972) *Models of Man*. The Hague: Martinus Hijhoff.

Dearden, R.F. (1986) 'Education, training and the preparation of teachers', in D.E. Cooper (ed.) *Education, Values and Mind: Essays for R.S. Peters*. London: Routledge and Kegan Paul.

Dewey, J. (1939) *Freedom and Culture*. New York: Putman.

Dewey, J. (1963) *Experience and Education* (revised edition). New York: Collier-Macmillan.

Dockrell, W.B. and Hamilton, D. (eds) (1980) *Rethinking Educational Research*. London: Hodder and Stoughton.

Dunlop, F.N. (1970) 'Education and human nature', *Proceedings of the Philosophy of Education Society of Great Britain*, **IV**, 32–44.

Eagleton, T. (1990) *The Significance of Theory*. Oxford: Basil Blackwell.

Eco, U. (1984) *The Name of the Rose* (trans. W. Weaver). London: Pan/Picador.

Elliott, J. (1978a) 'Classroom research: science or common sense?, in R. McAleese and D. Hamilton (eds) *Understanding Classroom Life*. Slough: NFER.

Elliott, J. (1978b) 'What is action research in schools?', *Journal of Curriculum Studies*, **10** (4), 355–7.

Elliott, J. (1980) 'Implications of classroom research for professional development', in E. Hoyle and J. Megarry (eds) *World Yearbook on Education, 1980: professional development of teachers*. London: Kogan Page.

Elliott, J. (1983) 'Teacher evaluation and teaching as a moral science', Cambridge Institute of Education, mimeo.

Elliott, J. (1987) 'Educational theory, practical philosophy and action research', *British Journal of Educational Studies*, **25** (2), 149–69.

Fay, B. (1975) *Social Theory and Political Practice*. London: Allen and Unwin.

Fay, B. (1987) *Critical Social Science: Liberation and Its Limits*. Cambridge: Cambridge University Press.

Feyerabend, P.K. (1975) *Against Method: Outline of an Anarchistic Theory of Knowledge*. London: New Left Books.

Filmer, P. *et al.* (1972) *New Directions in Sociological Theory*. London: Collier-Macmillan.

Foot, P. (1967) 'Introduction', in P. Foot (ed.) *Theories of Ethics*. London: Oxford University Press.

Foucault, M. (1970) *The Order of Things: an Archaeology of the Human Sciences*. London: Tavistock.

Freeman, H. and Jones, A. (1980) 'Educational research and two traditions of epistemology', *Educational Philosophy and Theory*, **12**, 1–20.

Gadamer, H.G. (1967) 'Theory, technology, practice: the task of the science of man', *Social Research*, **44**, 529–61.

Gadamer, H.G. (1980a) *Truth and Method* (trans. G. Bardey and J. Cummings). New York: Seabury Press.

Gadamer, H.G. (1980b) 'Practical philosophy as a model of the human sciences', *Research in Phenomenology*, **9**, 74–85.

Gadamer, H.G. (1981) 'What is practice?: the conditions of social reason', in H.G. Gadamer, *Reason in the Age of Science* (trans. F.G. Lawrence). Cambridge, MA: MIT Press.

Gauthier, D.P. (1963) *Practical Reasoning*. Oxford: Oxford University Press.

Geer, B. (1964) 'First days in the field', in P.E. Hammond (ed.) *Sociologists at Work: Essays on the Craft of Social Research*. New York: Basic Books, pp. 322–44.

Gellner, E. (1959) *Words and Things*. London, Gollancz.

Giddens, A. (1974) *Positivism and Sociology*. London: Heinemann.

Giddens, A. (1991) *Modernity and Self Identity*. Cambridge: Polity Press.

Gouldner, A. (1973) *For Sociology*. New York: Basic Books.

Gramsci, A. (1971) *Selections from the Prison Notebooks* (edited and trans. by Q. Hoare and G.N. Smith). London: Lawrence and Wishart.

Habermas, J. (1970a) *Towards a Rational Society* (trans. J. Shapiro). Boston, MA: Beacon Press.

Habermas, J. (1970b) 'Towards a theory of communicative competence', *Inquiry*, **13**.

Habermas, J. (1972) *Knowledge and Human Interests* (trans. J. Shapiro). London: Heinemann.

Habermas, J. (1974) *Theory and Practice* (trans. J. Viertel). London: Heinemann.

Habermas, J. (1979) *Communication and the Evolution of Society* (trans. T. McCarthy). London: Heinemann.

Habermas, J. (1984) *The Theory of Cummunicative Action, Vol. 1: Reason and the Rationalization of Society* (trans. T. McCarthy). Boston, MA: Beacon Press.

Habermas, J. (1987) *The Theory of Communicative Action, Vol. 2* (trans. T. McCarthy). Cambridge: Polity Press.

Hamilton, D. (1977) 'A methodological diary', in N. Norris (ed.) *Theory in Practice*. University of East Anglia, Centre for Applied Research in Education, pp. 136–46.

Hamilton, D. (1980) 'Educational research and the shadow of John Stuart Mill', in J.V. Smith and D. Hamilton (eds) *The Meritocratic Intellect: Studies in the History of Educational Research*. Aberdeen: Aberdeen University Press.

Hamilton, D., Jenkins, D., King, C., MacDonald, B. and Parlett, M. (1977) *Beyond the Numbers Game: a Reader in Educational Evaluation*. London: Macmillan.

Hanson, N.R. (1958) *Patterns of Discovery*. London: Cambridge University Press.

Hardie, C.D. (1942) *Truth and Fallacy in Educational Theory*. Cambridge: Cambridge University Press.

Hardie, C.D. (1957) 'On the concept of theory in education', *The Educands*, **3**, 1.

Hearn, F. (1985) *Freedom and Reason in Sociological Thought*. London: Allen and Unwin.

Hegel, G.F.W. (1952) *The Philosophy of Right* (trans. T.M. Knox). Oxford: Oxford University Press.

Hesse, M.B. (1978) 'Theory and values in the social sciences', in C. Hookway and P. Pettit (eds) *Action and Interpretation*. Cambridge: Cambridge University Press.

Hesse, M.B. (1980) *Revolution and Reconstruction in the Philosophy of Science*. Brighton: Harvester Press.

Hindess, B. (1977) *Philosophy and Methodology in the Social Sciences*. Hassocks, Sussex: Harvester Press.

Hirst, P.H. (1963) 'Philosophy and educational theory', *British Journal of Educational Studies*, **12**.

Hirst, P.H. (1966) 'Educational theory', in J.W. Tibble (ed.) *The Study of Education*. London: Routledge and Kegan Paul.

Hirst, P.H. (1973) 'The nature and scope of educational theory', in G. Langford and D.J. O'Connor (eds) *New Essays in the Philosophy of Education*. London: Routledge and Kegan Paul.

Hirst, P.H. (1974) *Knowledge and the Curriculum*. London: Routledge and Kegan Paul.

Hirst, P.H. (1983a) 'Educational theory', in P.H. Hirst (ed.) *Educational Theory and Its Foundation Disciplines*. London: Routledge and Kegan Paul.

Hirst, P. H. (ed) (1983b) *Educational Theory and Its Foundation Disciplines*. London: Routledge and Kegan Paul.

Hollis, M. (1977) *Models of Man*. Cambridge: Cambridge University Press.

Hopkins, D. (1985) *A Teacher's Guide to Classroom Research*. Milton Keynes: Open University Press.

Horkheimer, M. (1972) 'Traditional theory and critical theory', in M. Horkheimer, *Critical Theory*. New York: Seabury Press.

Hustler, D., Cassidy, A. and Cuff, E.C. (eds) (1986) *Action Research in Classrooms and Schools*. London, Allen and Unwin.

Illich, I. (1971) *Deschooling Society*. New York: Harper and Row.

Inglis, F. (1985) *The Management of Ignorance: a Political Theory of the Curriculum*. Oxford: Blackwell.

Jameson, F. (1984) 'Postmodernism or the cultural logic of late capitalism', *New Left Review*, **146**, 53–92.

Jay, M. (1973) *The Dialectical Imagination: a History of the Frankfurt School and the Institute for Social Research, 1923–50*. London: Heinemann.

Kant, I. (1959) 'What is Enlightenment?', in *The Foundations of the Metaphysics of Morals* (trans. L.W. Beck). Indianapolis, MN: Bobbs-Merrill.

Kant, I. (1963) *On History* (edited L.W. Beck). New York: Bobbs-Merrill.

Kekes, J. (1977) 'Rationality and problem solving', *Philosophy of the Social Sciences*, **7**, 351–66.

Kemmis, S. and McTaggart, R. (eds) (1988) *The Action Research Planner*, 3rd edn. Victoria: Deakin University Press.

Kolakowski, L. (1968) *The Alienation of Reason* (trans. N. Buterman). New York: Doubleday.

Kolakowski, L. (1972) *Positivist Philosophy*. Harmondsworth: Penguin.

Kuhn, T.S. (1970) *The Structure of Scientific Revolutions*. Chicago: Chicago University Press.

Lakatos, I. (1970) 'Falsification and the methodology of scientific research programmes', in I. Lakatos and A.E. Musgrove (eds) *Criticism and the Growth of Knowledge*. London: Cambridge University Press.

Langford, G. (1971) *Human Action*. London: Macmillan.

Langford, G. (1985) *Education, Persons and Society: a Philosophical Enquiry*. Basingstoke: Macmillan.

Langford, G. and O'Connor, D.J. (eds) (1973) *New Essays in the Philosophy of Education*. London: Routledge and Kegan Paul.

Laslett, P. and Runciman, W.G. (eds) (1967) *Philosophy, Politics and Society*. Oxford: Basil Blackwell.

Lewin, K. (1946) 'Action research and minority problems', *Journal of Social Issues*, **2** (4), 34–6.

Lewin, K. (1952) 'Group decisions and social change', in *The Action Research Reader*. Victoria: Deakin University Press (1988) pp. 47–56.

Lloyd, C. (ed.) (1983) *Social Theory and Political Practice*. Oxford: Clarendon Press.

Lobkowicz, N. (1967) *Theory and Practice: History of a Concept from Aristotle to Marx*. Notre Dame: University of Notre Dame Press.

Lobkowicz, N. (1977) 'On the history of theory and praxis', in T. Ball (ed.) *Political Theory and Praxis: New Perspectives*. Minneapolis: University of Minnesota Press.

McCarthy, T. (1975) 'Translator's introduction' to J. Habermas, *Legitimation Crisis*. Boston, MA: Beacon Press.

MacIntyre, A.C. (1967) *A Short History of Ethics*. London: Routledge and Kegan Paul.

MacIntyre, A.C. (1971) *Against the Self-images of the Age*. London: Duckworth.

MacIntyre, A.C. (1972) 'Is a science of comparative politics possible?', in P. Laslett, W.G. Runciman and Q. Skinner (eds) *Philosophy, Politics and Society*. Oxford: Basil Blackwell.

MacIntyre, A.C. (1981) *After Virtue: a Study in Moral Theory*. London: Duckworth.

MacIntyre, A.C. (1984) 'The relationship of philosophy to its past', in R. Rorty, J.B. Schneewind and Q. Skinner (eds) *Philosophy in History*. Cambridge: Cambridge University Press.

MacIntyre, A.C. (1988) *Whose Justice? Which Rationality?* London: Duckworth.

McKeon, R. (1952) 'Philosophy and Action', *Ethics*, **LXII**, 2.

Martin, J.R. (1961) 'On the reduction of "knowing that" to "knowing how" ', in B. Othanel Smith and R.H. Ennis (eds) *Language and Concepts in Education*. Chicago: Rand McNally.

Mills, C.W. (1959) *The Sociological Imagination*. Oxford: Oxford University Press.

Moore, T.W. (1974) *Educational Theory: an Introduction*. London: Routledge and Kegan Paul.

Moore, T.W. (1982) *Philosophy of Education: an Introduction*. London: Routledge and Kegan Paul.

Morris, B. (1972) *Objectives and Perspectives in Education*. London: Routledge and Kegan Paul.

Mundle, C.W.K. (1970) *A Critique of Linguistic Philosophy*. Oxford: Oxford University Press.

O'Connor, D.J. (1957) *An Introduction to the Philosophy of Education*. London: Routledge and Kegan Paul.

O'Connor, D.J. (1973) 'The nature and scope of educational theory', in G. Langford and D.J. O'Connor (eds) *New Essays in the Philosophy of Education*. London: Routledge and Kegan Paul.

Oakeshott, M. (1966) *Rationalism in Politics and Other Essays*. London: Methuen.

Outhwaite, W. (1975) *Understanding Social Life: the Method Called Verstehen*. London: Allen and Unwin.

Partridge, P. (1968) 'Politics, philosophy and ideology', in A. Quinton (ed.) *Political Philosophy*. London: Oxford University Press.

Peters, R.S. (1959) 'Must an educator have an aim?', in R.S. Peters, *Authority, Responsibility and Education*. London: George Allen and Unwin.

Peters, R.S. (1965) 'Education as initiation', in R.D. Archambault (ed.) *Philosophical Analysis and Education*. London: Routledge and Kegan Paul.

Peters, R.S. (1966a) *Ethics and Education*. London: Allen and Unwin.

Peters, R.S. (1966b) 'The philosophy of education', in J.W. Tibble (ed.) *The Study of Education*. London: Routledge and Kegan Paul.

Peters, R.S. (1973) 'Education as an academic discipline', *British Journal of Educational Studies*, **21**, 2.

Peters, R.S. (1977a) *Education and the Education of Teachers*. London: Routledge and Kegan Paul.

Peters, R.S. (1977b) 'Was Plato nearly right about education?', in R.S. Peters, *Education and the Education of Teachers*. London: Routledge and Kegan Paul.

Peters, R.S. (1977c) 'The justification of education', in R.S. Peters, *Education and the Education of Teachers*. London, Routledge and Kegan Paul.

Peters, R.S. (1979) 'Democratic values and educational aims', *Teachers' College Record*, **8** (3), 463–82.

Peters, R.S. (1983) 'Philosophy of education', in P.H. Hirst (ed.) *Educational Theory and Its Foundation Disciplines*. London: Routledge and Kegan Paul.

Phillips, D.C. (1971) *Theories, Values and Education*. Melbourne: Melbourne University Press.

Polanyi, M. (1973) *Personal Knowledge*. London: Routledge and Kegan Paul.

Popper, K.R. (1960) *The Poverty of Historicism*. London: Routledge and Kegan Paul.

Popper, K.R. (1969) 'The nature of philosophical problems and their roots in science', in *Conjectures and Refutations*. London: Routledge and Kegan Paul.

Popper, K.R. (1972) 'Two faces of common sense. An argument for common sense realism and against the common sense theory of knowledge', in *Objective Knowledge: an Evolutionary Approach*. Oxford: Clarendon Press.

Pring, R. (1977) 'Common sense and education', *Proceedings of the Philosophy of Education Society of Great Britain*, **11**, 57–77.

Putnam, H. (1974) 'The primacy of practice', in P.A. Schilpp (ed.) *The Philosophy of Karl R. Popper*. La Salle: Open Court.

Putnam, H. (1981) *Reason, Truth and History*. London: Cambridge University Press.

Quinton, A. (1975) 'Has man an essence?', in R.S. Peters (ed.) *Nature and Conduct*. London: Macmillan.

Reid, W.A. (1978) *Thinking about the Curriculum*. London: Routledge and Kegan Paul.

Rorty, R. (1979) *Philosophy and the Mirror of Nature*. Princeton, NJ: Princeton University Press.

Rorty, R. (1982) *Consequences of Pragmatism*. Minneapolis: University of Minnesota Press.

Ryan, A. (1970) *Philosophy of the Social Sciences*. London: Macmillan.

Ryle, G. (1949) *The Concept of Mind*. London: Hutchinson.

Sanford, N. (1970) 'Whatever happened to action research', *Journal of Social Issues*, **26** (4), 3–23, republished in (1988) *The Action Research Reader*, Victoria: Deakin University Press.

Scheffler, I. (1967) *Science and Subjectivity*. New York: Bobbs-Merrill.

Schon, D.A. (1983) *The Reflective Practitioner: How Professionals Think in Action*. London: Temple Smith.

Schwab, J.J. (1969) 'The practical: a language for curriculum', *School Review*, **78**, 1–24.

Schwab, J.J. (1974) 'Decision and choice: the coming duty of science teaching', *Journal of Research in Science Teaching*, **11**, 309–17.

Searle, J.R. (1972) *Speech Acts*. Cambridge: Cambridge University Press.

Skinner, Q. (1980) 'Language and social change', in L. Michaels and C. Ricks (eds) *The State of the Language*. Berkeley: University of California Press.

Smart, B. (1993) *Postmodernity*. London: Routledge.

Smith, B.O., Stanley, W.O. and Shores, J.H. (1950) *Fundamentals of Curriculum Development*. New York: World Books.

Squires, J. (ed.) (1993) *Principled Positions: Postmodernism and the Rediscovery of Value*. London: Lawrence and Wishart Ltd.

Stanley, W.O., Smith, B.O., Benne, K.D. and Anderson, A.W. (1956) *Social Foundations of Education*. New York: Dryden.

Stenhouse, L. (1975) *An Introduction to Curriculum Research and Development*. London: Heinemann.

Stenhouse, L.A. (1979) 'The problem of standards in illuminative research', *Scottish Educational Review*, **11** (1), 7.

Taylor, C. (1967) 'Neutrality in political science', in P. Laslett and W.G. Runciman (eds) *Philosophy, Politics and Society*. Oxford: Basil Blackwell.

Taylor, C. (1984a) 'Hegel, history and politics', in M. Sandel (ed.) *Liberalism and Its Critics*. Oxford: Blackwell.

Taylor, C. (1984b) 'Philosophy and its history', in R. Rorty, J.B. Schneewind and Q. Skinner (eds) *Philosophy in History*. Cambridge: Cambridge University Press.

Thomas, D. (1979) *Naturalism and Social Science*. Cambridge: Cambridge University Press.

Tibble, J.W. (ed.) (1966) *The Study of Education*. London: Routledge and Kegan Paul.

Toulmin, S. (1972) *Human Understanding*. Princeton, NJ: Princeton University Press.

Toulmin, S. (1990) *Cosmopolis: the Hidden Agenda of Modernity*. New York: The Free Press.

Touraine, A. (1981) *The Voice and the Eye: an Analysis of Social Movements*. Cambridge: Cambridge University Press.

Travers, R.M.W. (1969) *An Introduction to Educational Research*. London: Macmillan.

Van Manen, M. (1977) 'Linking ways of knowing with ways of being practical', *Curriculum Inquiry*, **6**, 205–28.

Verma, G.K. and Beard, R.M. (1981) *What is Educational Research?* Aldershot: Gower.

Von Wright, G.H. (1971) *Explanation and Understanding*. London: Routledge and Kegan Paul.

Warnock, M. (ed.) (1962) *John Stuart Mill*. London: Fontana.

Weber, M. (1964) *The Theory of Social and Economic Organization*. New York: The Free Press.

Westbrook, R.B. (1991) *John Dewey and American Democracy*. Ithaca, NY: Cornell University Press.

Williams, B. (1972) *Morality: an Introduction to Ethics*. Cambridge: Cambridge University Press.

Wilson, J. (1975) *Educational Theory and the Preparation of Teachers*. Slough: NFER.

Wilson, P.S. (1971) *Interest and Discipline in Education*. London: Routledge and Kegan Paul.

Winch, P. (1958) *The Idea of a Social Science*. London: Routledge and Kegan Paul.

Winch, P. (1971) 'Human nature', in *The Proper Study: Royal Institute of Philosophy Lectures*. London: Macmillan.

Winter, R. (1987) *Action Research and the Nature of Social Inquiry: Professional Innovation and Educational Work*. Aldershot: Gower.

Winter, R. (1989) *Learning from Experience: Principles and Practice in Action Research*. Lewes: Falmer Press.

Wittgenstein, L. (1963) *Philosophical Investigations* (trans. G.E.M. Anscombe). Oxford: Blackwell.

Wolin, S. (1972) 'Political theory as a vocation', in M. Fleisher (ed.) *Machiavelli and the Nature of Political Thought*. New York: Atheneum.

Woods, J. and Dray, W.H. (1973) 'Aims of education – a conceptual enquiry', in R.S. Peters (ed.) *The Philosophy of Education*. Oxford: Oxford University Press.

Young, M.D.F. (ed.) (1971) *Knowledge and Control: New Directions for the Sociology of Education*. London: Macmillan.

INDEX